A Christmas Compendium

A Christmas Compendium

J. John

continuum

Continuum

The Tower Building   15 East 26th Street
11 York Road   New York
London SE1 7NX   NY 10010

www.continuumbooks.com

First published 2005

British Library Cataloguing-in-Publication Data
A catalogue record for this book is available from the British Library.

ISBN 0–8264–8749–1

Designed and typeset by Ben Cracknell Studios
Printed and bound in Great Britain by MPG Books Ltd, Bodmin

Contents

Acknowledgements

I owe special gratitude to my niece Rachel Ioannou, Sarah Doyle and to Chris Moffat, who assisted me in my research and helped disentangle the many conflicting facts behind our Christmas traditions. And I thank my wife Killy for reading the first draft of the manuscript and helping me to refine and shape it.

And finally I thank God. He could not make himself bigger to impress us, so he made himself smaller to attract us.

Introduction

———————

Would you prefer an eighteenth-century mince pie (including hares, pheasants, rabbits, pigeons, partridges, eggs, pickled mushrooms and spices) to one you could pick up in a supermarket?

Would you believe that Christmas could be cancelled – the mince pies, church services and even the Christmas tree?

Do you value your Ferrero Rocher chocolate as much as it might have been valued by the Aztecs, who used cocoa beans as a form of currency?

Christmas is a time of anticipation, celebration and, as I have discovered while writing this book, many surprises. I set out to unravel the mysteries and myths of our Christmas traditions, delving into the birth of Christ as well as into many customs dating back to the dawn of civilization. In doing so I found myself amused, appalled, astonished and fascinated. It is my hope that this will be your experience too. Have a very merry – and altogether more enlightened – Christmas.

Advent

*The first season of the Church year, leading up to Christmas
and including the four preceding Sundays.*

Origin: from the Latin adventus, *meaning 'arrival'.*

The modern Advent period is marked by the opening of chocolate calendars. Their designs vary greatly, ranging from traditional Nativity scenes to characters from *The Simpsons*. Some families celebrate the occasion by lighting an Advent candle at mealtimes.

Originally, however, the Advent season was a time of strict fasting, observed in anticipation of the festival marking the birth of Jesus Christ. The first mention of the Advent season was at the Council of Tours in AD 567, when a fast for monks in December was recorded. At the close of the sixth century, Gregory the Great of Rome adopted the rule of fasting for the four Sundays in Advent, and in the following century it became a well-known practice in the West to set aside these days. In the Greek Church, 40 days of fasting are observed before Christmas. Today it is seen as a remarkable feat of self-control if someone restricts him- or herself to one chocolate a day from the calendar.

Advent is a time to look forward to Christmas and it is an opportunity to reflect on the reason for the season. Christians believe that Advent is a time to prepare our hearts for Christ, just as we prepare our homes for Christmas.

Alleluia

Variant of the word 'Hallelujah', meaning 'God be praised'.

Origin: from the Greek alleluia, *or directly from the Hebrew* hallelujah, *meaning 'praise ye the Lord'.*

This is a word we often sing in Christmas carols without ever stopping to think what it really means. In Luke's Gospel in the Bible the author explains how the shepherds 'praised God' after they had seen Jesus in Bethlehem. In contemporary churches this word is used regularly in worship as Christians recognize both the need to praise God as their King and the delight they receive from doing this.

Angels

*A spiritual being believed to act as an attendant or messenger of
God, conventionally represented as a human form with wings.*

Origin: from the Greek angelos, *meaning 'messenger'.*

We still dramatize the part that angels played at the first Nativity
scene with children appearing in their school plays wearing white
sheets and tinsel haloes.

Luke's Gospel tells how, before Jesus' birth, the angel Gabriel informed
Zechariah of John the Baptist's birth. Shortly after, Gabriel was sent by
God to tell Mary she would be the mother of Jesus. An angel appeared
to the shepherds to tell them the 'good news' of Jesus' arrival. An angel
also appeared to Joseph, telling him to flee to Egypt with Mary and the
baby Jesus because Herod was planning to kill all the boys under the age
of two. Christian tradition holds that, although unnamed, it was Gabriel
who also appeared in these last two situations. In Hebrew Gabriel means
'God is my strength'.

We often think of angels as sweet and inoffensive. After all, the angels
in the Gospel stories said, 'Do not be afraid . . .'. Whilst these angels were
kind, this should not diminish the important task they were sent to
perform, which was to pass on messages from God. And any illusions of
angels being 'sweet' are also blown out of the water by a close look at the
Gospel accounts, which show that when an angel arrived people were
'terrified'. This will come as no surprise when we read other accounts
of angels in the Bible: 'His face shone like the sun, and his feet were
like pillars of fire . . . he gave a great shout like the roar of a lion . . .'
(Rev. 10.1–3).

The earliest images of winged angels date back to the early Egyptians,
and the Ancient Greeks also painted divine beings with wings. As
Christianity grew, so did the number of theories about angels. Some early
writers even tried to calculate how many angels existed. In the fourteenth
century, for example, there were believed to be 301,655,722 angels.

Today many people speak of having a 'guardian angel' to keep them from harm. In a 2004 MORI poll, 43 per cent of people questioned said they had experienced a guardian angel. The footballer David Beckham has a tattoo of an angel on his neck. But is this belief in the protective responsibility of angels well founded? The Bible tells us in the Psalms that God does send angels for our protection, but whether or not every individual has a specific 'guardian angel' is not stated. In a different way, Christians believe that in worship they are joining with the great assembly of angels in praising God.

Annunciation

The announcement of the incarnation by the
angel Gabriel to Mary.

The account of the angel Gabriel's visit to Mary is well known, because it is usually included in school Nativity plays. In the Gospel of Luke we read of God's instruction to Mary: "'Don't be afraid, Mary,'" the angel told her, "for you have found favour with God! You will conceive and give birth to a son, and you will name him Jesus. He will be very great and will be called the Son of the Most High. The Lord God will give him the throne of his ancestor David. And he will reign over Israel forever; his Kingdom will never end!'" (Lk. 1.30–33). Mary was an ordinary Jewish teenager. She, and the world around her, would have deemed her life to be fairly insignificant. Yet Gabriel told her how she was highly favoured with God.

Mary could not understand how, as a virgin, she could give birth to a baby, but the angel promised that the Holy Spirit would make this possible. Often today we fear the miraculous and through science we endeavour to rationalize everything. Yet clearly God acted supernaturally to carry out his plans.

When Mary had recovered from her shock at Gabriel's announcement, she replied with these remarkable words: 'I am the Lord's servant. May everything you have said about me come true.' (Lk. 1.38). Ever since the first Christmas, Mary has been revered and respected by generations for her humble yet strong and obedient faith.

Balthasar

Origin: means 'protect the king' in Phoenician.

In the Bible, the wise men who came to visit the baby Jesus are not referred to as kings, but as Magi. An apocryphal tradition in the West gives them the names Caspar, Melchior and Balthasar. It was during the Middle Ages that the three kings became popular and today their part in the Christmas story is re-enacted by crown-wearing children in Nativity plays. Balthasar is said to have been the monarch of Ethiopia, the land of spices.

Syrian Christians gave Persian names to the wise men, and Balthasar was known to them as Gushnasaph. The name means something like 'as energetic and virile as a horse', or 'full of desire for having horses'. This may sound very strange to our Western understanding of a wise man.

Balthasar is said to have given Jesus the gift of frankincense in a special container called a censer. Frankincense (from the French, meaning 'pure incense') is the dried resin of Boswellia trees, which at the time of Christ grew in Arabia, India, Somalia and Ethiopia. It was necessary to strip the bark, cut into the wood and wait for the tree to 'bleed' liquid, which was ultimately turned into resin. This painstaking process meant that frankincense was in short supply, though demand was high because it had varied and important uses. Consequently, prices were also high. The ancient Egyptians used frankincense to treat wounds, create perfumes, and as a fragrance to mask the repulsive fumes of cremated bodies.

In addition, frankincense was a critical ingredient used in worship in the Temple in Jerusalem, representing the prayers of Israel lifting up to God in heaven. Balthasar's gift can be seen as a foreshadowing of Jesus being the one to open communication between humankind and God, enabling us to know our Father again. As frankincense was a precious substance at the time of Jesus' birth, the gift also showed Christ's worthiness to be treated as a king.

Banning of Christmas

Doesn't it seem like an awful idea that anyone would want to ban Christmas? Yet this is exactly what happened in seventeenth-century England. Christmas had been lavishly celebrated in the Tudor and Stuart courts, but the Puritans in Great Britain and America were appalled by the revelry of Christmas customs and sought to eliminate the celebration. Oliver Cromwell and his parliament abolished Christmas in England on 3 June 1647. The act which abolished Christmas read, 'No observation shall be had of the five-and-twentieth day of December; nor any solemnity used or exercised in churches upon that day in respect thereof.' For 13 years parliament sat on Christmas Day and soldiers ensured shops were kept open and churches were closed. Evergreens were banned and mince pies outlawed because they were seen as temptation to wickedness and overindulgence. In Massachusetts, America, Puritan leaders made the celebration of Christmas illegal between 1659 and 1681. One law stated that 'whosoever shall be found observing such a day as Christmas shall pay five shillings as a fine'.

Despite government efforts, many people continued to celebrate the holiday in the privacy of their homes. In opposition, more than 10,000 people from Kent signed a petition and demanded that 'if they could not have their Christmas Day, they would have the King back on the throne'. In 1660 the Royalists returned and Charles II was put on the throne. The festival of Christmas came back. It was a welcome return to a great many people and it has been with us ever since.

Baubles

A decorative hollow ball hung on a Christmas tree.

Origin: from the French baubel, *meaning 'child's toy'.*

In 1867, when gas came to Lauscha (a town in the Thuringian mountain area in Germany), glassblowers were able to use constantly hot yet adjustable gas flames. They began to experiment with the production of very delicate, thin glass shapes. They developed these into glass ball ornaments called *Kugeln*, which were used to decorate houses during the festive season. The earliest shapes were fruits, such as grapes, apples and pears, or pine cones. In the 1840s immigrants from Germany to America used their skills to develop the concept, and by 1870 the technique of silvering the insides of the baubles was established, so that they were more reflective. In the 1890s F.W. Woolworth, the founder of the convenience store, discovered the sale potential of these ornaments and made annual trips to Lauscha. In 1909 he bought 216,000 ornaments there. By the 1950s, plastic, foil and styrofoam were the materials used for mass-produced ornaments, though demand for the traditional blown-glass baubles has increased in recent decades, as they have become something of a collector's item.

Bells

*A hollow object, typically made of metal and in the shape of a
deep inverted cup, that sounds like a musical note when struck.*

Origin: from the Germanic bellan, *meaning 'to bellow'.*

The use of large church bells to call people to worship may have been started by Bishop Paulinus of Nola (*c.* 431 AD) in Campania, Italy.

High in the towers, suspended between heaven and earth, bells represent communication between God and his people.

New church bells have been dedicated and even baptized before being used. One legend states that the townspeople of Lochen in Holland neglected to baptize two church bells, and one day the devil grabbed these bells and buried them at the bottom of two ponds outside the town. Even today, it is said that these bells can on be heard ringing at midnight on Christmas Eve. In other European towns, the story goes that if you put your ear to the ground on Christmas Eve you will hear the ringing of bells from churches that were swallowed up by earthquakes during worship services.

Before we had television and radio people were given news after the ringing of church bells. In Scandinavia, bells still ring at 4 p.m. on Christmas Eve to signal that Christmas has started and people can leave work.

Bethlehem

The town of Jesus' birth.

Origin: Hebrew meaning 'house of bread'.

The people of Israel waited a long time for Jesus the Messiah to arrive. The prophets in the Old Testament of the Bible prophesied that the Saviour would be born in Bethlehem. Five hundred years before the birth of Christ, the Prophet Micah wrote: 'But you, O Bethlehem Ephrathah, are only a small village among all the people of Judah. Yet a ruler of Israel will come from you, one whose origins are from the distant past' (Mic. 5.2).

According to the Gospels, when Mary and Joseph arrived in Bethlehem there was no room for them at the inn and they had to use a stable, which was a shelter for the animals. Another Old Testament prophecy states that 'an ox knows its owner, and a donkey recognizes its master's care – but Israel doesn't know' (Isa. 1.3). How ironic that even the ox and the donkey recognized Jesus as the Messiah, but Israel did not. As paintings came to be a way of depicting the Nativity, the ox and the donkey became part of the story of the stable and the baby Jesus.

These days, Christmas comes three times each year to the city of Bethlehem. While the Western Church follows the Gregorian calender (introduced in 1582) and celebrates Christmas on 25 December, the Russian Church still uses the old Julian calendar, which places the celebration on 7 January. The Armenian Church celebrates on 6 January.

Emperor Justinian built Bethlehem's Church of the Nativity in the sixth century over the ruins of an older church built by the Emperor Constantine and his mother, St Helena. That church had been built to replace a temple to the Greek god Adonis. All of these structures were built over a series of caves that were considered to be the location of Christ's birth. The church was nearly destroyed by invading Persians in the seventh century, but they stopped when they came upon a mural of the Magi that depicted the kings in Persian dress. There is a 14-pointed silver star marking the location of the original manger. The Turkish Sultan donated it after a previous star had disappeared. The floor around it is marked in Latin: *Hic De Virgine Maria Jesus Christus Natus Est*, meaning, 'Here of the Virgin Mary, Jesus Christ was born'.

Boar's head

The boar's head ceremony was a pagan custom that remained popular in Britain and Scandinavia until the 1600s. The pagan Norsemen used to kill a boar during the winter solstice and offer its head to their goddess of agriculture and fertility, in the hope that she would bless the spring crops of the following year. One of the earliest Christmas carols printed in English is the 'Boar's Head Carol', found in a book dating from 1521 and written by Wynkyn de Worde (what a name!). The carol was written after a supposed battle between a boar and a student of Queen's College, Oxford. According to the story, a student called Mr Copcot took a walk one day in Shotover Forest with his nose buried in a book by the Ancient Greek writer Aristotle. Suddenly a wild boar ran out and attacked him and, as Copcot had no time to draw his sword, he instinctively rammed the book into the boar's mouth so that it choked to death. He then cut off the boar's head and carried it back to the college in triumph.

At Queen's College the boar's head ceremony goes back over 500 years, and it still occurs today. The head is now made of jellied meats pressed into a mould and decorated with rosemary, bay and holly, and an orange is placed in the boar's mouth. It is carried on a platter into the great hall by four people, ahead of whom walk the choir, singing the old carol:

> The boar's head in hand I bear,
> Bedeck'd with bays and rosemary;
> And I pray you, my masters, be merry . . .

After the dish has reached the table, the orange is given to the chief singer and the sprigs of rosemary and bay to the guests.

Even before the incident at Queen's, boar's head was traditionally eaten at Christmas in the Middle Ages, and this lasted until the seventeenth century, when wild boar became almost extinct in Britain.

Boxing Day

A public holiday on the first day after Christmas Day.

———————————

Everyone knows they are guaranteed a cold turkey sandwich on Boxing Day as families coordinate the eating up of the Christmas Day food. For many people Boxing Day is spent trekking across the country to visit the relatives they did not see on Christmas Day, while others spend it in front of the television watching an annual repeat classic. Setting apart a further day's rest after Christmas is an old British tradition, but was only made an official holiday in 1871. It is also known as St Stephen's Day, named after the first Christian martyr who was stoned to death. St Stephen is the patron saint of horses, which is why there are so many traditional race meetings on Boxing Day. It also used to be a day earmarked for charitable giving. In the village of Drayton Beauchamp in Buckinghamshire there was a tradition of 'Stephening', when villagers went to the vicar's house and expected to be given as much bread, cheese and ale as possible – for free! One year the vicar refused to give the traditional 'Christmas box' and in disgust the parishioners broke into the manse and ate as much as they could find anyway. As the parish expanded the tradition died out, and it had ended by 1834.

The name Boxing Day comes partly from the alms boxes kept in churches to collect money for the needy, which were opened after Christmas so that resources could be shared amongst local people. Also, artisans and apprentices had clay boxes, which they would take to their master's customers and ask for money. On Boxing Day the pottery boxes were smashed and the money spent by the artisans on food and drink.

Brandy butter

A stiff sauce of brandy, butter and sugar.

One traditional way to cope with an unappealing Christmas pudding is to smother it with brandy butter or brandy sauce. Here is a recipe:

125g unsalted butter
250g sieved icing sugar
brandy to taste

Soften the butter and beat until smooth, either by hand or with an electric mixer. Gradually add the sieved icing sugar and then add as much or as little brandy as you like. Allow to set in the fridge and use on whatever festive food you like.

WARNING: Not to be used in conjunction with any calorie-counting diet.

Brussels sprouts

A vegetable consisting of the small compact bud of a variety of cabbage which bears many such buds along a tall single stem.

Eating Brussels sprouts has commonly been one of the trials of Christmas for children – and many adults. Yet, despite our distaste for sprouts and the fact that we rarely eat them at any other time of the year, we couldn't imagine a Christmas dinner without them.

Brussels sprouts are members of the brassica family and are therefore kin to broccoli as well as cabbage. They grow in bunches of 20 to 40 on the stem of a plant between two and three feet tall. They are low in fat and high in antioxidants, provided you don't overboil them. They are one of the most nutritious vegetables around, packed full of vitamin C, folic acid, beta carotene, vitamin E and iron. Sprouts taste bitter because they use that taste as a chemical weapon to ward off insects. Brussels sprouts were named after the capital of Belgium, where they may have been cultivated first, and have been mentioned in books since 1587.

On 10 December 2003, Britain's Dave Mynard ate 43 Brussels sprouts in one minute at the Cactus Television Studios in London. If you want to beat the record, here are the rules:

1. This record is based on the number of commercially available (cooked) Brussels sprouts eaten in one minute using a wooden toothpick/cocktail stick.

2. Only one Brussels sprout can be spiked and eaten at a time.

3. The Brussels sprouts must be put on a plate, which is then placed on a table in front of the seated contestant.

4. The plate has to remain on the table at all times while the Brussels sprout is being spiked and brought to the mouth.

5. An adequate supply of drinking water should be on hand for the contestant.

6. Only wholly eaten Brussels sprouts count towards the final total.

7. At least one timekeeper should monitor the event with a highly accurate stopwatch.

Caesar Augustus

'Caesar' was the title given to the Roman emperors.

Origin: family name passed on from Roman statesman Julius Caesar.

―――――――――――

Caesar Augustus was Julius Caesar's grand-nephew and was originally called Octavian. He came to power when Julius Caesar was assassinated. In his will, Julius Caesar left all his possessions, including the throne, to his grand-nephew. Octavian was so successful that he was renamed Augustus, meaning 'venerable', and he became the first Roman emperor, ruling from 27 BC to AD 14. Augustus was responsible for the Pax Romana, the era of peace between all the different parts of the Roman Empire, which covered most of southern Europe and the Mediterranean. He took the title of Pontifex Maximus, which means 'highest priest'. When Jesus was born, Augustus was the most powerful leader in the known world.

Luke's Gospel records how Augustus issued a decree that a census be taken of the entire Roman world. Joseph and Mary (who was pregnant with Jesus) had to leave Nazareth and travel the 70 miles to Bethlehem to register because it was Joseph's ancestral home (Lk. 2.1). Although we don't know how they travelled to Bethlehem, riding a donkey would have been a likely mode of transport. This gruelling journey is captured very sweetly by the popular children's song 'Little Donkey'.

The census was taken in order to collect taxes, to fund the lavish Roman lifestyle and resource the thousands of soldiers maintaining the Empire at home and abroad. We know from another source, *The Acts of Augustus*, that Augustus rated the three censuses he conducted as the eighth greatest achievement of his rule.

Calendar

A chart or series of pages showing the weeks and months of a particular year; a system by which the beginning, length and subdivisions of the year are fixed.

Origin: from the Latin kalendae, *meaning first day of the month (when the order of days was proclaimed).*

The Bible does not record the date of Jesus' birth as the writers either did not know or did not consider the date important. The early Christians thought the world would end very soon and so were not concerned with celebrating Christ's birthday. Before long, however, Christians realized the Church might remain on earth for a while and so how Christians would commemorate Jesus' life became more important. A few dates for Jesus' birth were considered as Roman thinkers tried to schematize science and history. Pagans of the Roman Empire celebrated the birthday of Sol Invictus, the 'unconquered sun god', on 25 December and many identified this god with Mithras, a popular pagan deity at the time of Christ. When Christianity became the accepted religion of the Roman Empire in AD 312, the Church decided to celebrate Christ's birthday on 25 December – a day to celebrate the unconquerable Son.

Candles

*A cylinder of wax or tallow with a central wick which
produces light as it burns.*

Origin: from the Latin candere, *meaning 'be white or glisten'.*

In our electricity-dependent culture we forget that one of the main
reasons why candles are so much part of Christmas is that in the
Western world the festival occurs at the darkest time of year. Long ago,
ancient peoples in Europe became unsettled when the days grew shorter
because the sun, which they believed was a god and the source of all
warmth, light and life, was 'hiding' itself. During the solstice (literally 'the
sun stands still' in Latin) the ancients could not fathom if the sun would
return to help them or not. In response they made their own lights, in
bonfires, lanterns and candles, in order to 'encourage' the sun to shine.

Early Christians tried to shake off the pagan association with candles
but still used them for illumination and decoration. Candles played a
largely functional role in lighting churches for evening services, which the
Christians thought was appropriate considering that Jesus is referred to as
'the light of the world' in the Gospels.

Before electric lights were invented, candles were placed on Christmas
trees as decoration. Beeswax was expensive, so these candles were made of
tallow (animal fat) which spluttered and smoked when burning. Legend
has it that Martin Luther, founder of the German Protestant Church, was
the first person to put candles on a Christmas tree. Obviously tree candles
were far from safe. One nineteenth-century magazine recommended to its
readers that a 12 foot (3m) Christmas tree should have no more than 400
candles! Having said that, Christmas trees were usually only cut on
Christmas Eve, so they would have been more moist and less likely to
catch fire. Some safety devices were invented, but with little success. In
1867 an American called Charles Kirchhof created a candle-holder with a
weight on the bottom to help the candle stand upright. Unfortunately,
the weight often caused the candle to slide off the branch. More
successful was Frederick Artz, another American, who invented a candle-
holder with a spring clip that could attach to the branch. This was made

of tin and had a little cup at the bottom to catch melted wax. Such holders can still be purchased today.

Victorian candles were generally moulded as spirals because, as the wax on smooth-sided candles melted, it would drip down the side of the candle and onto the floor. With a spiral candle it did not matter if the candle was leaning, because the liquid wax would run down through the spiral without dripping.

There is something very atmospheric about a church lit with candles, and today they are often used in Midnight Mass services to help people reflect on the idea of Jesus coming into the world. Many Christians would maintain that Jesus has 'lightened' up their lives and brought them from utter darkness to a place where they can 'see' clearly again.

Candlemas

A Christian festival held on 2 February to commemorate the purification of the Virgin Mary and the presentation of Christ in the Temple.

Origin: Old English candelmaesse, *the custom of bringing candles to the church to be blessed by the priest.*

In many traditions 2 February has been a significant date, falling midway between the winter solstice and the spring equinox. The Celts celebrated Imbolc on this day, a pagan festival anticipating the planting of crops and birth of farm animals.

The date also comes 39 days after Christmas Day, and in the sixth century was declared the feast of the Purification of Mary. According to the Jewish tradition, women went through a purification ceremony 40 days after the birth of a male child. The earliest records of this festival show that it was originally held on 14 February, 39 days after Epiphany (which commemorates the visit of the Magi). Perhaps this date (Valentine's Day) is not known so much for the purification of a virgin today . . .

The festival came to be known as Candlemas due to the inclusion of lighted candles in the proceedings, symbolic of Jesus Christ the light of the world. It has a rich and diverse history and is also known as the Festival of Lights. In the East the emphasis of the day's observances is on Christ, and in the West it is on the Virgin Mary. As the Catholic Church developed, Candlemas became the day on which the year's supply of candles for the church was blessed.

Today, following the popularity of the 1993 film *Groundhog Day* starring Bill Murray, some Americans recognize 2 February as 'Groundhog Day'. The origin of this day dates back to the 1700s, when German settlers arrived in Pennsylvania bringing the traditional Candlemas Day with them. Superstition held that animals such as badgers and bears would break their hibernation on 2 February and pop their heads out into the open air. If it was cloudy, then it would be good weather for the next six weeks. If it was sunny when the groundhogs peeped out of their winter quarters, they would see their shadow and would go back to sleep for a further six weeks while wintry weather prevailed. This tradition was combined with the indigenous Delaware Indians' beliefs that groundhogs were their honourable ancestors, thence the name Groundhog Day.

Since 1887, a small town in Pennsylvania named Punxsutawney has been host to a staged appearance of a selected groundhog. Weathermen and newspaper photographers alike attend this event, along with the general public who use it as an excuse to celebrate! The organizers of this event claim that the animal is never wrong in its predictions, but an examination of the records shows the groundhogs to be merely 40 per cent accurate. Since the release of the movie *Groundhog Day*, attendance at the event has grown. There have been up to 35,000 visitors gathered on 2 February in Punxsutawney, over five times the town's population.

Candy cane

*A stick of striped sweet rock with a curved end,
resembling a walking stick.*

One of the most common symbols of Christmas, especially in America, is the candy cane. Not only are candy canes used as a sweet Christmas treat, they are also used for decoration. But how did this seasonal candy get its familiar shape, and when did it become part of Christmas tradition?

At Cologne Cathedral in Germany, pageants used to be an important part of the Christmas celebrations. In about 1670 the choirmaster had sticks of candy bent into the shape of a shepherd's crook and passed them out to children who attended the ceremonies. This became a popular tradition, and eventually the practice of passing out sugar canes at such ceremonies spread throughout Europe.

The idea of hanging candy canes on Christmas trees had made its way to America by the 1800s. At that time, however, they were still pure white. They are represented this way on Christmas cards made before 1900, and it is not until the early twentieth century that the canes appear with their familiar red stripes.

Many people have given religious meaning to the shape and form of the candy cane. Of course, its shape is like the letter 'J' and is therefore said to reflect Jesus' name. It is also in the shape of a shepherd's crook, symbolic of how Jesus, known as the 'Good Shepherd', watches over his followers. The flavour of peppermint is similar to another member of the mint family, hyssop. In the Old Testament hyssop was used for purification and sacrifice, and this is said to symbolize the purity of Jesus and the sacrifice he made on the cross. The bold red stripe represents God's love and the blood spilled at Jesus' crucifixion.

Cards

*Piece of card for writing on, especially a
postcard or greetings card.*

Origin: from Greek khartes, *meaning 'papyrus leaf'.*

As early as 1822, the postmaster in Washington, DC was worried by the amount of extra mail at Christmas. Even though commercial cards were not available at that time, people were already sending so many homemade cards that 16 extra postmen had to be hired in the city. His preferred solution to the problem was to limit by law the number of cards a person could send. 'I don't know what we'll do if this keeps on,' he wrote!

The first commercial Christmas card was sent in 1843 by Sir Henry Cole and had three illustrations, two scenes called 'clothing the naked' and 'feeding the hungry', and one depicting a family enjoying Christmas. This card was sent in the midst of the Industrial Revolution, when behind the benefits of a developing economy lay social dislocation and abject poverty. Henry Cole, the first director of London's Victoria and Albert museum, sympathized with these social problems but also recognized that industrialization was irreversible. He tried to ensure that British products were beautiful and functional to conquer the international market. His Christmas card was an attempt to bring quality design to day-to-day objects. Although he produced 1,000 of these cards, however, the printers sold them for 1 shilling each, which was expensive at the time, and they did not sell well. The poor sales could also be put down to the fact that one of the pictures showed a mother handing a wine glass to her young daughter and the image was seen as irresponsible.

The idea of Christmas cards did not catch on immediately, and only in the 1860s did printers begin producing them en masse. In 1870 the introduction of the halfpenny stamp for postcards gave the Christmas card trade a boost, yet still the practice of sending cards was confined to the upper and middle classes until the 1880s, when manufacturers began producing them for a few pence per dozen.

Today a wide range of 'charity' Christmas cards can be bought, and part of the money spent on the card goes towards a charitable cause. In addition, many shops compete for the most original designs or messages, while in the last decade demand has soared for the novelty of a handmade card. Radio programmes and children's TV often run annual competitions to find the worst or most tasteless card!

An edition of *The Times* in 1883 summed up why the sending of Christmas cards became so popular:

> *The wholesome custom has been frequently the happy means of ending strifes, cementing broken friendships and strengthening family and neighbourhood ties in all conditions of life . . .*

Carols

Religious song or popular hymn associated with Christmas.

Origin: from the Greek choros, *meaning dancing in a circle, and from Old French* carole, *a secular ring-dance with song, passed into the English language c.1300.*

———————

The earliest carols involved dancing as well as singing. A leader would sing a line or verse while the dancers stayed still. At the refrain the 'chorus' would dance and sing, moving in a circle with linked hands, the rhythm marked with clapping and stamping. The themes of these 'caroles' were often concerned with politics or love. With the arrival of Christianity in Britain, however, dancing was frowned upon – especially in church – because of its association with pagan ritual. Many church people therefore provided alternative religious lyrics for popular secular carols to reform the raucous singing and dancing. By the fourteenth century the emphasis was clearly on singing in worship as opposed to dancing, and carols were dominated by religious lyrics.

The first formal collection of carols was by Wynkyn de Worde. Entitled *Christmasse Carolles*, it was printed in 1521. During the Protestant Reformation carols were repressed and lay dormant for decades, being passed on only through oral tradition. The nineteenth-century Anglican Revival brought with it great interest in old Christmas traditions and many of the clergy tried to reintroduce carols in church worship. Men such as Dr John Mason Neale and Rev George Ratcliffe Woodward translated many Latin carols into English, into the form we sing today.

From 1850 onwards many new carols were written. They were published in 1871, in a collection called *Christmas Carols Old and New*. Carols such as 'Silent Night', 'Once in Royal David's City' and 'Away in a Manger' are from this time. By the end of the century the carol was integral to Christmas and its use was encouraged in religious services.

Probably the most famous of all carols is 'Silent Night', composed by the organist Franz Gruber (1787–1863) to verses by Rev Joseph Mohr, the village priest of Oberndorf, Salzburg, Austria. The story goes that on Christmas Eve 1818 the church organ was found to be faulty because mice had eaten through the bellows. In desperation Joseph Mohr brought a poem to the organist and asked if he could arrange it for choir and guitar. He could and he did. The carol continues to be a Christmas classic.

Another well-known carol with an interesting history is 'Hark the Herald'. Charles Wesley originally wrote this carol in 1739, with slow and solemn music to go with his lyrics. Over a hundred years later Felix Mendelssohn composed a cantata which the English musician William H. Cummings adapted to fit the lyrics of 'Hark the Herald'. This is the tune we sing today. Mendelssohn said the tune was suitable for sacred words and described the piece as 'soldierlike and buxom'.

There is something in carols of great depth and sentimentality. Although they can appear antiquated in their form and wording, they somehow seem to act as a common language for us all.

Carol service

A Christmas carol service is an enduringly popular occasion. It almost always includes readings taken from the Gospels which tell the story of Jesus' birth. In between these the congregation sing popular carols, often heartily and with much vigour. In many places these services are held by candlelight to create an atmosphere of wonder as we celebrate the birth of a Saviour.

The most well-known form of carol service is the 'Festival of Nine Lessons and Carols', first introduced in 1880 by the clergyman (and later archbishop) Edward White Benson. The service was conducted at 10 p.m. on Christmas Eve, and it is said that this time was chosen in order to 'get the men out of the pubs early so they would not be drunk for the midnight service'. It was later adapted for use in King's College, Cambridge by Eric Milner-White when he became Dean in 1918, in response to a need for more imaginative Church worship. This particular service became famous when the BBC began to broadcast it annually in the late 1920s. It remains a fixture in christmas broadcasting schedules today.

When we celebrate birthdays we don't usually retell the story of the person's birth at their party. We don't recall details about the pregnancy, or about the feelings and thoughts of Mum and Dad when they heard they were going to have a baby. Yet every Christmas we sing carols about Jesus' birth and retell all the 'baby-talk' details that have been passed down to us.

Carol singers

To go 'carolling': to sing carols in the streets.

Before carol singing in public became popular, there were official carol singers called 'Waits'. These were bands of people often directed by local council leaders, who were the only ones in the towns and villages with power to take money from the public. (If others did this, they were sometimes charged as beggars!) They were called 'Waits' because they only sang on Christmas Eve, which was sometimes known as 'Watchnight' or 'Waitnight', remembering the shepherds who were watching their sheep when the angels appeared to them.

As new carols became popular, so did the custom of singing carols round the streets. Today singers may still come to our doors, but more frequently groups of people sing in public places such as a shopping centre or marketplace, or round a communal Christmas tree.

Caspar

Origin: means 'treasurer' in Persian.

Caspar, the 20-year-old King of Tarsus, was considered to be one of the three wise men known as the Magi. He is said to have brought Jesus myrrh in a gold-mounted horn. Myrrh is a gum resin from trees found in Africa and Arabia. The tree called 'Commiphora' or 'DinDin' produces the sap when the bark is cut, and when the myrrh hardens it is usually made into a powder. At the time of Jesus' birth myrrh was very valuable. In addition to being used in perfumes and incense, it was also used in ointment for embalming by the Egyptians and as a medicine for sores and wounds.

Jesus himself would be embalmed with this perfume after he was crucified. Many see this gift pointing forwards to the most significant part of Jesus' life – his death on the cross. At Golgotha, before he was crucified, Jesus was offered 'wine drugged with myrrh, but he refused it' (Mk 15.23). This drink had an anaesthetic effect, and would have helped to lessen the pain of crucifixion.

The wise men were powerful figures in their own right, but it is significant that when the Magi presented their gifts to the baby Jesus, they bowed down and worshipped him.

Charity

The voluntary giving of money to help those in need.

Origin: from the Latin caritas, *from* carus, *meaning 'dear'.*

———————

Many shops sell charity Christmas cards during the festive period containing a greeting and some information about the charity. There are literally thousands of different charity Christmas cards to choose from and they comprise about one-fifth of all the cards sent internationally at Christmas. The first charity card was produced in 1949 by the United Nations International Children's Emergency Fund (UNICEF) and was designed by seven-year-old Jitka Samkova from Rudolfo in Czechoslovakia, a town that had been badly damaged in World War II. In gratitude for the assistance UNICEF had given the town, Jitka painted a picture of people dancing with joy. She used a piece of glass to paint on, as she had no paper.

Christmas originally became a time for charitable giving through generous tipping. In the late Middle Ages, the well-off were obliged at Christmas to open their doors to the less fortunate and provide them with food and drink. However, many wealthy people did not want to open their homes to the poor and many would plan to be away at Christmas to avoid the obligation to give to social inferiors. Sometimes the poor would knock on the doors of wealthy homes offering simple entertainment for money, such as a verse recital, a short drama or a song.

As Europe and the US experienced industrialization, ad hoc giving became less effective. The gap between the growing middle class and the abject poor (who lived in slums) was growing. Victorian organizations (charities) aimed to bridge this gap and spend contributions more efficiently than individuals could.

At Christmas time, newspapers and magazines tended to focus on the 'worthy' poor, especially women and children, and the power of the press to evoke pity helped raise funds for the poor. An early Christmas edition of *Punch* in 1843 contained Thomas Hood's 'Song of the Shirt' which fiercely denounced sweated industries. More recently, organizations such as Crisis at Christmas open from 23 to 30 December each year to provide an alternative family for many homeless and vulnerably housed people who feel particularly lonely over the Christmas period.

Many people endeavour to make Christmas boxes to send to children in needy places. These gift-filled shoeboxes bring joy and hope to children in desperate situations around the world.

Charities of all kinds tend to intensify fundraising activities at Christmas since, as Charles Dickens wrote, 'It is a time, when Want is keenly felt, and Abundance rejoices.'

Cherubim

A winged angelic being described in biblical
tradition as attending on God, conventionally represented
as a chubby child with wings.

Origin: from the Hebrew kerub, *meaning 'one who intercedes'.*

From paintings and traditional Christmas cards, we can all recall images of those baby-faced angels, often blowing pipes or flying around. But where have these images come from? The Bible passages relating to cherubim give us an amazing array of representations. They are, variously, guardians of the garden of Eden, creatures upon whom God rides the winds, winged creatures with four faces – of a cherub, a man, a lion and an eagle – and worshippers in God's throne room. That's quite a line-up of images, and most of them do not even begin to resemble the popular concept of a cherub. The traditional artistic impressions do, however, capture something of innocence, childhood, humanity and the divine – themes that are central to the humble birth of Mary's child in Bethlehem. It may be on account of this that cherubim are often associated with the Christmas season.

Chocolate

A food made from roasted and ground cacao seeds,
typically sweetened and eaten as confectionery.

Origin: Old Spanish xocolatl, *meaning 'bitter water'.*

———————————

Christmas is a time for eating chocolate – lots of it. Manufacturers make the most of the increased demand for chocolate at Christmas and provide us with specially wrapped boxes. In addition, there is the arrival of the customary selection box for children.

The earliest record of chocolate was over 1,500 years ago in the South American rainforests, which had the ideal climate for cultivation of the plant from which chocolate is derived – the cacao tree. The Aztecs prized the beans and acquired them through trade and the spoils of war. The beans were so valuable that they were used as currency: 100 beans bought a turkey.

'Xocolatl', or 'chocolat' as it became known, was first brought to Europe by Hernán Cortés (1485–1547), soon after which the first chocolate factories were opened in Spain. There the dried fermented beans brought back from the New World by the Spanish fleets were roasted and ground, and by the early seventeenth century chocolate powder was being exported to other parts of Europe.

The first 'chocolate house' in England opened in London in 1657 and was followed rapidly by many others. Initially popular as a drink, chocolate was first eaten in solid form when bakers in England began adding cocoa powder to cakes in the mid-1600s. In 1828 a Dutch chemist, Johannes Van Houten, invented a method of extracting the bitter-tasting fat or cocoa butter from the roasted ground beans. His aim was to make the drink smoother and more palatable, but he unknowingly paved the way for solid chocolate as we know it today.

Some of the most famous names in chocolate were Quakers – a peaceful Christian community who for centuries held a virtual monopoly of chocolate-making in the English-speaking world. Cadbury, Fry and Rowntree are probably the best-known manufacturers. Because of their pacifist convictions, Quakers were prohibited from most normal business activities, but as an industrious people with a strong belief in a work ethic, they involved themselves very successfully in food-related businesses. Cadbury have stayed with chocolate production and are now one of the most widely known chocolate makers in the world. From their earliest beginnings in business the Quakers were noted for their enlightened treatment of their employees, providing not just employment but everything the workers needed to better themselves, including good housing.

Much debate surrounds our craving for chocolate. It could be something to do with the fact that every 100g of chocolate contains 660mg of phenyl ethylamine, a chemical relative of amphetamines that has been shown to produce feelings of wellbeing and alertness. Perhaps that is why we particularly like to binge on chocolate at Christmas.

Christingle

*A lighted candle symbolizing Christ, held by
children at Advent services.*

Origin: from German dialect Christkindl,
meaning 'Christchild'.

The first Christingle service was held in Marienborn, Moravia, in 1747
when the minister, John de Wattville, wanting to find a new way of
telling the Christmas story to children, gave each child a lit candle tied
with a red ribbon. He asked them to light the candles at home and place
them in their windows to show the light of Christ to passers-by. The
tradition was kept alive by the Moravian Church and in the United
Kingdom was adopted by the Children's Society in the 1950s as a way of
raising awareness of their work.

Many churches and schools now hold Christingle services at any time
from Advent to the end of the Epiphany season. Each child is helped to
take an orange (representing the world) and insert four cocktail sticks
into it (representing the four seasons). Fruit, nuts and sweets can then be
attached to the cocktail sticks to represent the fruits of the earth. A red
ribbon is then tied around the centre of the orange as a reminder that
Christ died for us all. Finally, a small lighted candle is fixed on top to
symbolize Jesus Christ, the light of the world.

Christmas cake

A rich fruitcake covered with marzipan and icing.

Origin: 'cake', denoting a small flat bread roll.

There's nothing quite like a slice of rich Christmas cake on Christmas Day afternoon. The old-fashioned Twelfth Night cake was close to what we would now call a Christmas cake. Sometimes these were of phenomenal size – like the one advertised in 1811:

> *Extraordinary Large Twelfth Night Cake, 18 feet in circumference, to be seen at Adam's, 41 Cheapside, opposite Wood Street. The cake considerably surpasses in size any that had been made in London, or, in fact, in the world: its weight is nearly half a ton, and actually contains nearly two hundred and a half weight of currants and upwards of one thousand eggs. This wonderful cake is ready for inspection!*

The predecessor of the Christmas cake was a fine cake made with the finest milled wheat flour, baked only in the great houses back in the fourteenth century as not many people had ovens. It was a rich fruitcake recipe with a topping of marzipan or almond paste, and was used to celebrate the Easter and Christmas festivities. However, where the Easter cake was plain, the Christmas one contained dried fruits and spices representing the exotic spices of the East and the gifts of the Magi.

Twelfth Night is on 5 January and is traditionally the last day of the Christmas season. It used to be a time for having a great feast, and the cake was an essential part of the festivities. In great houses a dried bean and a pea were baked into the cake, one in each half. The cake was decorated with sugar, like our modern icing but not so dense, and ornamentation. As the visitors arrived for the feast they were given a piece of the cake, ladies from the left side and gentlemen from the right. Whoever got the bean became 'king of the revels' for the night, and everyone had to do as he said. The lady who won the pea was his 'queen' for the evening. In smaller homes the cake was a simple fruitcake with a bean in it, which was given to guests during the 12 days of Christmas. Whoever got the bean was supposed to be a kind of guardian angel for that family for the year, so it was an important task and usually it was arranged that a senior member of the family would receive the bean.

As Twelfth Night is the eve of the Christian festival of Epiphany, it was marked by some kind of religious observance: a visit to the church, a service of some kind. After the Reformation, however, these customs were banned by the Puritans and fell into disuse. Without its religious overtones, Twelfth Night became a time of mischief and overindulgence. In 1870 Queen Victoria announced that she felt it was inappropriate to hold such an un-Christian festival, and Twelfth Night was banned as a feast day. The confectioners who made the cakes were left with boxes full of figurines and models for Twelfth Night cakes, and they had lost revenue through the banning of the feast. So they began to bake fruitcakes and decorate them with snowy scenes, or even flower gardens and romantic italianate ruins. These they sold not for 5 January, but for Christmas parties in December. And that is why we have the ever-popular Christmas cake.

Christmas Day

The annual Christian festival celebrating Christ's birthday and held commonly on 25 December.

Origin: 'Christmas', Old English Cristes Maesse, meaning 'Mass of Christ'.

Every family has its own particular Christmas customs and routines. There will be people we always see on Christmas Day, be they relatives or good friends. Some people open presents early, before church or lunch, while others wait till the afternoon and enjoy their gifts while they digest their dinner.

The original name for Christmas, Cristes Maesse, was first written in a Saxon book in 1038. The name literally meant 'the mass of Christ', as originally Christmas was celebrated through religious worship as well as feasting. Three main church services had evolved by the eleventh century: Midnight Mass, remembering the angelic appearance; the Mass at Dawn, commemorating the visitation of the shepherds; and the Day Mass, celebrating the coming of God's Son, the Christ. Today Christmas Day celebrations vary widely across the world. Here are just a few facts about Christmas Day in other lands.

Ukrainians prepare a traditional 12-course meal for the day. A family's youngest child watches through the window for the evening star to appear, a signal that the feast can begin. In Holland on Christmas Day there is usually a special breakfast including a fruit loaf or *kerstbrood*, and people will eat *kersttulband*, a traditional Christmas cake with a hole in the middle. In France, following Midnight Mass, families often return home or visit a restaurant for a grand Christmas feast known as the *reveillon*, which includes delicacies such as oysters, lobster and a roast truffled turkey. After the *reveillon* children will put shoes, slippers or boots in front of the fire for Père Noël (Father Christmas) to fill with gifts.

In Japan, only about 1 per cent of the population is Christian, but Christmas is celebrated as a non-religious holiday. It began on 24 December 1955, when the Japanese government announced that the food shortages caused by World War II were officially over and a crowd of 1.5 million packed Ginza, the most exclusive shopping district in Tokyo. Ever since, Christmas has been celebrated in Ginza and, as a result of Western influences, the figure of Santa Claus has become increasingly well known.

Christmas Eve

The day before Christmas Day.

Origin: from 'even', meaning 'evening', of Germanic origin.

———————

There is something magical about Christmas Eve. The family tends to unite when work has finished and children wait expectantly for the big day to arrive full of its treats and surprises. Since the time of the angels' visit to the shepherds 'by night' at the first Christmas, Christmas Eve has been charged with anticipation.

In Scandinavia the main Christmas celebration is on Christmas Eve, when families and friends enjoy a big meal together. There will almost certainly be a *smorgasbord*, a fine collection of meat and fish dishes.

In Britain many still attend a Midnight Mass, a service including communion and reflecting on the coming of Jesus over 2,000 years ago. In keeping with the wonder of this day, in 1968 the crew of Apollo 8 sent a Christmas Eve message to the millions on earth watching the flight. In turn they read the first five verses of the book of Genesis, 'In the beginning God created the heavens and the earth . . .'. It ended with Frank Borman saying, 'And from the crew of Apollo 8 we close with goodnight, good luck, a Merry Christmas and God bless all of you – all you on the good earth.'

Christmas Island

There are two Christmas Islands in the world. The first is a dot in the Indian Ocean and even though it is in Australian territory, its closest neighbour is Java, 360km away. It comprises the summit of an oceanic mountain, rising to 361m above sea level and predominantly covered by tropical rainforest.

British and Dutch navigators first included the island on their charts in the early seventeenth century and Captain William Mynors named the island when he arrived on Christmas Day 1643, although he was unable to land. In 1688, when Captain William Dampier landed at the Dales (on the West Coast), two of his crew became the first recorded people to set foot on Christmas Island. Christmas Island was not settled until 1888, when the Clunies-Ross brothers from the neighbouring Cocos-Keeling Islands (some 900km to the south-west) established a settlement at Flying Fish Cove to collect timber supplies. The British Admiralty annexed the island on 6 June 1888, and phosphate extraction became the impetus behind the island's development.

Today the recoverable reserves of phosphate are nearly exhausted, and during the 1990s a shift in economy began to take place whereby other industries such as tourism edged their way in. A recent population survey showed fewer than 2,000 inhabitants, only one third of whom are female. Almost three quarters of the population are from Chinese origins, but all are Australian citizens and the Australian schooling system prevails. An interesting place indeed.

The other Christmas Island is one of the many islands in the Republic of Kiribati. Part of the Line Island Group, it is the largest coral atoll in the world with an area of 248 square miles. Its population is mainly Micronesian from the I-Kiribati archipelago, with a small group of Polynesians from Tuvalu and some expatriates. From the time of the Cold War, Christmas Island will be remembered for the nuclear bomb tests that took place off its coast. Britain's first nuclear test explosion at Christmas Island took place on 15 May 1957, and in November 1957 there were two further H-bomb explosions.

Christmas pudding

A rich boiled pudding eaten at Christmas,
made with flour, suet and dried fruit.

Origin: Old French boudin, meaning 'black pudding'.
From Latin botellus, meaning 'sausage, small intestine'.

Christmas pudding seems to be one of those foods you either love or hate. It has its origins from the early days of Christianity, when porridge was eaten on Christmas Eve to line the stomach after the day's fasting. Gradually people added spices, dried fruits and honey to the porridge to make it a special dish for Christmas. In the Middle Ages it was turned into a pudding called frumenty. The mixture was so stiff with all the fruits that they would tie it in a cloth, place it in a large cauldron of boiling water and boil it for many hours. It was also sometimes called plum pottage, meaning a mixture as thick as porridge. In the seventeenth century the word 'plum' referred to raisins or other fruits – plum pudding has in fact never contained plums.

In Tudor times Christmas pudding was a combination of meat, oatmeal and spices all boiled together. This mixture was then wrapped in pig guts so that the pudding looked like a sausage and could be sliced.

Often homemade puddings would include silver charms and new coins. Whoever found the charm in their piece of pudding would have good luck in the year to come. This tradition dates right back to ancient Rome and the Saturnalia feast, when it was customary to place a dried bean inside a cake. Whoever found the bean was 'king' for the evening and was able to order other guests to make fools of themselves in a game of dares. This continued until the Victorian era.

Christmas puddings have traditionally contained brandy and been set alight for a few seconds before serving. The largest Christmas pudding recorded in *The Guinness Book of Records* weighed 1,390kg. A company called Herbert Adams in Australia made it in 1987 and it took three weeks to prepare the ingredients.

Church

A building used for public Christian worship.

Origin: from Greek kuriakon (doma),
meaning 'Lord's (house)'.

———————————

Many people traditionally gather at church on Christmas Eve for Midnight Mass. Christians see Christmas as the most important Christian festival after Easter, and so on Christmas Day they go to church to worship God for sending his Son Jesus.

Interestingly, an English law passed in 1551 stated that everyone must go to church on Christmas Day on foot. The law has never been repealed, so technically everyone going to church by bike or car on Christmas Day is breaking the law.

Commercialism

Emphasis on maximizing profit.

———————————

As early as the eighteenth century advertisements for holiday presents appeared in European magazines, but the explosion of Christmas commercialism took place in the nineteenth century. In 1897 the playwright George Bernard Shaw showed concern about this: 'Christmas is forced upon a reluctant and disgusted nation by shopkeepers and the press; on its own merits it would wither and shrivel in the fiery breath of universal hatred.'

In Victorian times businesses became more assertive in attracting people with manufactured presents and promotional gimmicks developed. A description of a typical Victorian street market can be seen in Henry Mayhew's *London Labour and London Poor* (1851):

The crowd is almost impassable. Indeed the scene in these parts has more of
the character of a fair than a market. There are hundreds of stalls and every
stall has one or two lights . . . The crisp Christmas air is filled with the
calls of the stall-holders, 'Chestnuts all 'ot, a penny a score [twenty]' bawls
one. 'Fine warrnuts [walnuts], sixteen a penny' screams another . . .

Since then Christmas has become increasingly commercial each year. Now Christmas cards and presents can be found in shops as early as August, when the consumerist Christmas 'machine' kicks into action.

A poll conducted by the Center for a New American Dream (CNAD) found that 84 per cent of respondents wanted a less materialistic Christmas season. In the UK, according to MORI, the three things that the public find most stressful over Christmas are thinking up gift ideas, buying gifts and financial concerns.

Christmas shopping in overcrowded shops, slaving away in the kitchen, present wrapping late at night, credit card bills. Bah humbug! Christmas is often a time when its true meaning gets lost in the rush and bustle of postmodern life. Let's revive the true meaning of Christmas and keep our sanity.

Crackers

Decorated paper cylinder which, when pulled apart, makes
a sharp noise and releases a small toy or other novelty.

Origin: onomatopoeia — i.e. the word is like the sound.

———————————

The first picture of a Christmas cracker appeared in the *Illustrated London News* in 1847. It was an English invention, but was influenced by French packaging and Chinese custom.

On a trip to Paris a London confectioner called Tom Smith saw sweets called 'bonbons' wrapped in twists of paper. He brought back the idea, put slips of paper in the wrappers and called them 'love mottoes', hoping that young men would buy them for their sweethearts. With time the idea caught on and later little paper hats, tokens and small toys were also placed inside the wrappers. One year, as Smith was standing by the fire listening to the crackling, he decided to put a 'cracker' strip inside the 'bonbons' so that when pulled from either end they would make a snapping noise.

Crackers were originally called 'cosaques', because the sound they made when pulled apart was reminiscent of the noise made by Cossack horsemen as they galloped past, cracking whips. Crackers have remained popular for over a century and show no sign of losing favour.

Often crackers will include a colourful paper hat to wear during Christmas dinner. The idea of such a hat goes right back to pagan superstition. It was said that evil forces constantly threatened the sun's survival, especially during the winter solstice. As evil could only be fought with evil, assuming the guise of the devil was thought to drive away any real devils. In those early pagan celebrations, hats and masks were decorated in a more sinister way, but a remnant of the tradition continues in our modern paper hats.

The largest functional cracker ever made was 45.72m (150ft) long and 3.04m (10ft) in diameter. It was made by the international rugby league player Ray Price and was pulled in the car park of Westfield Shopping Town, Chatswood, Sydney on 9 November 1991.

Crib

A model of the Nativity of Christ.

Origin: from Germanic krebe, *meaning 'basket'.*

Perhaps the earliest Christmas crib was the one used by Pope Sixtus III around AD 400. He introduced the idea of Midnight Mass on Christmas Eve in Rome and in the church of Santa Maria Maggiore he built a copy of Jesus' crib. The practice of 'visualizing' the Nativity scene became popular in 1223 when Francis of Assisi found a cave near the village of Greccio and placed there an ass, an ox and a carved figure of a baby, lying in a manger. The Franciscan monk wanted to communicate the reality of the birth of Christ, in all its poverty and discomfort, to ordinary people. Families from all over the region heard what he had done and visited the site. Another saint, Bonaventure, writing in the thirteenth century, describes how St Francis came up with the idea:

That this might not seem an innovaton, he sought and obtained licence from the supreme pontiff, and they made ready a manger, and bade hay, together with an ox and an ass, be brought unto the place. The man of God (St Francis) filled with tender love, stood before the manger, bathed in tears, and overflowing with joy. Solemn masses were celebrated over the manger, Francis chanting the Holy Gospel.

In the eighteenth century the creation of Christmas cribs was taken very seriously and in Naples the finest sculptors and painters were employed to cut the figures and decorate them. The Bavarian National Museum at Munich has a fine collection of cribs from various periods and various lands – including Germany, Italy and Sicily – which show the elaborate care that was taken in preparation of these models.

Cribs can now be seen in most churches and in many shops and public buildings. There is a permanent underwater crib in Amalfi, Italy, where life-sized figures have been arranged in a Nativity scene on the seabed. At a special exhibition of cribs in France in 1966 a 'space crib' was set up in which the Nativity scene was set on a distant planet and the three wise men were shown arriving in a rocket.

Dancing

To dance: move rhythmically to music, typically following a set sequence of steps.

Origin: from Old French dancer, *of unknown origin.*

In Europe there has always been a great winter festival dramatizing the passing of the old year and the beginning of the new. When the sun seemed to be disappearing, the celebrations were an attempt to appease the mysterious forces of nature and encourage the sun back out to bring fertility to the land. The two most important midwinter festivals of the later Roman Empire were Saturnalia and the Kalends. The northern European festival of Yuletide had similarities to these southern festivals and the Germanic tribes enjoyed feasting, wassailing and carousing. Carols in twelfth-century France were amorous ring-dances. These spread to England and between the thirteenth and sixteenth centuries carols were a mixture of singing and dancing.

The aspect of celebration from these early festivals continued into Tudor times and despite the creative endeavours of the church to 'Christianize' Christmas, it retained its secular nature. The twelve days of Christmas were a national holiday, observed with much indulgent feasting, singing and dancing. The Tudor age marked the height of this indulgence, before the Puritans attempted to abolish the 'irreverent' celebration of Christmas. The royals, however, were not to be inhibited from showing what they could do on the dance floor. Queen Elizabeth I was said to have danced at Christmas: 'The head of the Church of England was to be seen in her old age dancing three or four galliards.'

Dickens, Charles

Charles Dickens (1812–1870) was best known for his distinctively cruel, comic and repugnant characters. He remains the most widely read of the Victorian novelists.

Astonishing though it may seem, in the early part of the nineteenth century Christmas had become almost extinct. *The Times* newspaper did not mention Christmas once between 1790 and 1835. Charles Dickens was instrumental in 'reviving' Christmas during the Victorian era.

Dickens' childhood was not a happy one. His father had an inability to stay out of debt, which led to his imprisonment in 1824. Dickens was sent out to a blacking warehouse and memories of conditions there haunted him for the rest of his life. In defiance of his parents' failure to educate him, Dickens worked hard, first as a clerk in a solicitor's office and then as a reporter of parliamentary debates for the *Morning Chronicle*. His talent for portraits and caricatures was discovered there and his work became immensely popular.

Dickens wrote *A Christmas Carol*, his best-known Christmas book, in 1843, for two reasons. First, he wrote it as a response to the economic climate in a decade called the 'hungry forties' in England, when thousands of workers were unemployed and famine was widespread in the north. One in every eleven people in England and Wales was a pauper and reports told of abusive conditions in the workplace. *A Christmas Carol* attempted to uncover some of these conditions and challenge wealthier people and the government to act with compassion and generosity. Second, the book was written for personal reasons. The financial uncertainty and poverty Dickens had known enabled him to write realistically about the uneducated and downtrodden. The character of Ebenezer Scrooge embodied a callous disregard for others.

In addition, Dickens needed money to support his wife and four children. His publishers, who had been losing faith in his work, had angered Dickens, so he paid for the production of the book himself. It took him only two months to write, after which he claimed it was 'the greatest I thing I have ever achieved'. He wrote in December 1843: 'I have endeavoured in this little book to raise the ghost of an idea, which shall not put my readers out of humour with themselves, with each other, with the season or with me. May it haunt their houses pleasantly . . .'

The book was a huge success and after its publication on 17 December 1843 the first printing of 6,000 copies sold out in a matter of days. By the end of the year, 15,000 copies had been sold and in 1844 alone, nine London theatres staged dramatized versions of the story. However, the price of the book was low and Dickens did not enjoy the large reward he had desired, by 1844 only acquiring a fifth of his estimated £1,000 return. Yet with time he earned £45,000 from his readings and left a considerable estate to his children.

A British silent film of the story was made in 1908, followed by an American one in 1910, and in 1970 there was a technicolour musical version starring Albert Finney. *A Christmas Carol* is still produced on the stage and in film today, including modern versions such as *Scrooged*, starring Bill Murray.

Dickens loved Christmas. As he put it in his *Sketches by Boz*, 'A Christmas family party! We know nothing more delightful!' He returned to the theme again and again in his works and he brought together nostalgia for a colourful past and anxiety for the moral and social problems of his day. Christmas in Dickens' novels stands as a metaphor for human sympathy and its appeal is associated with childhood, family and tenderness. The 'Dickensian' Christmas was an illumination of both the contentment and anxieties of the Victorian middle classes. This section of society was growing in prosperity thanks to social and economic change, yet was apprehensive about change because of the dislocation of traditional values. Today we look at the age of Dickens as a time when Christmas really was Christmas, yet through his writing he was in fact reviving the 'ideal' Christmas of the past.

Egypt

A country in Northern Africa, bordering the
Mediterranean Sea.

Origin: from the Greek Aigyptos, meaning
'the river Nile, Egypt'.

Egypt was a unified kingdom that arose around 3200 BC and was ruled by a series of dynasties for the following three millennia. The last native dynasty fell to the Persians in 341 BC and they were replaced in turn by the Greeks, Romans and Byzantines.

Following the birth of Jesus and the visit of the Magi, an angel appeared to Joseph in a dream telling him to escape to Egypt as Herod was planning to search for Jesus and kill him. Herod thought Jesus, this child 'king', was a threat to his kingdom. Joseph must have been fearful, yet he trusted in God, took Mary and Jesus and escaped in the night to Egypt. They stayed there until Herod's death when another angel appeared to Joseph in a dream telling him it was safe to return to Israel.

According to the Hebrew Scriptures, Egypt had been a place of slavery for God's people, the Jews, and it was into Israel that God led them during the great exodus when they escaped from that servitude. By contrast, in the story of Jesus, we see that Egypt is a place of refuge for God's Son, from the dangers in Israel. As with the rest of the Christmas story, general perceptions are turned upside down, and we find the goodness of God in the most unexpected places.

Elizabeth

Mother of John the Baptist, wife of Zechariah.

Origin: Hebrew, meaning 'consecrated to God'.

The Bible records that Elizabeth was very old. Her husband Zechariah was a priest, and one day when he was working in the temple an angel appeared to him saying that his wife Elizabeth would have a son called John. Zechariah must have thought God was kidding. A child? At their age? He said, 'How can I be sure this will happen? I'm an old man now, and my wife is also well along in years' (Lk. 1.18). I wonder what Elizabeth would have thought about that last comment?

Because of his unbelief (for which we can hardly blame him) the angel told Zechariah he would not be able to speak until the day John was born. Upon returning home, he managed to communicate to Elizabeth what would happen, and she did indeed become pregnant. When Mary was told she would be the mother of Jesus, it was Elizabeth she went to visit and as excited mothers together they awaited the birth of their babies. When John was born, Elizabeth's family wanted to call him Zechariah after his father, but Zechariah, who still could not speak, scrawled on a writing tablet, 'His name is John', and immediately he was able to speak again. Later John the Baptist went on to prepare the way for Jesus' arrival.

In a similar way to Mary, Elizabeth was significant because she was an ordinary Jewish woman who had no titles or special status, yet was chosen by God to do something incredibly important. She and her husband Zechariah played vital roles in the story of Jesus' birth, the first Christmas.

Epiphany

The manifestation of the divine nature of Christ to the Gentiles as represented by the Magi; the festival commemorating this on 6 January.

Origin: from the Greek epiphainein, *meaning 'reveal'.*

Like many Christian celebrations, Epiphany has its roots in the ancient world. In Egypt at the time of the Pharaohs 6 January was a sacred day to mark the overflowing of the River Nile, which flooded its banks annually and made the land fertile again.

Epiphany is the last day of the twelve days of Christmas. It is generally seen as the official end of the Christmas season and marks the day when Christmas decorations are traditionally taken down.

Epiphany commemorates the revelation to the Magi of Jesus as the son of God. From the Middle Ages until the mid-nineteenth century, Twelfth Night (Epiphany) was more popular than Christmas Day. Indeed, Eastern Orthodox churches, for example the Armenian Church, still celebrate Epiphany as the most important day of the Christmas season and for them it commemorates the baptism of Christ.

In 1330 King Edward I of England made offerings of gold, frankincense and myrrh in his royal chapel on Epiphany. Until the reign of George III in the eighteenth century, the monarch always attended this ceremony. The service is still held at the Chapel Royal in St James's Palace in London, and offerings are made on behalf of Queen Elizabeth.

Feast of Fools

*Feast: a large meal, especially a celebratory one;
a religious celebration.*

Origin: from Latin festus, *meaning 'joyous'.*

The medieval Feast of Fools was held between Christmas and Epiphany, often on New Year's Day. The chief location of the festivities was the church itself, and the principal organizers were the lower clergy. The idea of the feast was the inversion of status and the performance by inferior clergy of duties normally carried out by their superiors. The celebrations were relics of the ancient ceremonies of birth and renewal which took place at New Year and involved a temporary overturning of all values.

The feast was widely celebrated throughout cathedrals and collegiate churches in France, England, Flanders, Germany and Bohemia. Most of the customs can be traced back to ancient pagan festivals like Saturnalia and the January Kalends. In a time when there were no such things as secular holidays, the Feast of Fools was a church-approved form of the modern April Fool's Day – a chance to give folly its annual outing. As the Theological Faculty in Paris argued in 1440, defending the Feast of Fools, 'even a wine vat would burst if the bung-hole were not opened occasionally to let out the air'.

A similarly spirited ritual more common in Britain was that of the 'boy-bishop', taking place on Holy Innocents' Day (28 December) or sometimes on St Nicholas' Day (6 December). A choirboy would be elected to play the bishop's role, and other boys also gained status and were dressed up as deans, archdeacons and canons. These child 'bishops' would preside over religious ceremonies dressed in the bishops' regalia, lead processions, preach and carry out tours to bless people and raise money. Sometimes the boy bishop made the adult cathedral dignitaries act as taper- and incense-bearers so that the great were clearly seen to perform the functions of the lowly.

Figgy pudding

You've heard the Christmas carol 'We Wish You a Merry Christmas', but have you ever wondered what the second verse is about? What does 'Now bring us some figgy pudding' actually mean? This is the dish that Mary Cratchit serves her family for Christmas dessert in Charles Dickens' *A Christmas Carol*. It is of similar origins to the popular Christmas pudding, and some say that it did not even contain figs originally, only currants and raisins.

Here's a recipe (adapted a little) from Mrs Beaton herself, England's famous traditional writer of cookery books.

125g dried figs, chopped
125g flour
125g applesauce
200g breadcrumbs
1 teaspoon baking powder
200g sugar
1 teaspoon nutmeg
1 teaspoon cinnamon
1 teaspoon ginger
1 cup orange juice
1 cup dried or canned cranberries

Mix all the ingredients together thoroughly. Place in a closed container in a large pot of boiling water. Steam the pudding for at least two and a half hours, or until it is rather firm. You might want to serve it with some kind of sauce or vanilla pudding, but it is delicious plain.

Forgiveness

To forgive: stop feeling angry or resentful towards someone for an offence or mistake.

Origin: of Germanic origin, related to 'for' and 'give'.

———————————

Forgiveness isn't easy. No one would list it among their 'Top Ten Things to Do'. Indeed, forgiveness is so difficult that after some people have been wronged they fail to forgive for a whole lifetime. They can never quite let go of the grievance that someone or some incident has caused them. In comparison, where instances of genuine forgiveness occur, it is truly humbling and could be seen as one of the noblest acts a human being can perform.

The forgiveness offered by God through his Son Jesus is the most genuine and earth-shattering forgiveness of all. At Christmas we celebrate the birth of Jesus, who died 33 years later as a substitute for each one of us, taking the punishment for every wrong committed by the whole of human kind.

This anonymous poem sums up why God sent Jesus.

If our greatest need had been information,
God would have sent us an educator.
If our greatest need had been money,
God would have sent us an economist.
If our greatest need had been technology,
God would have sent us a scientist.
If our greatest need had been pleasure,
God would have sent us an entertainer.
But our greatest need was forgiveness,
So God sent us a Saviour.

Just before Leonardo da Vinci began painting the *Last Supper*, he argued bitterly with a fellow painter. He was so angry he decided to paint the face of Judas Iscariot as this 'enemy'. In this way, the hated painter's face would be preserved for ages in the face of the disciple who betrayed Jesus. He painted quickly and was delighted that people noticed whose face he had created. Da Vinci then tried to paint Jesus' face, but something seemed to be stopping him. In time, he saw that his hatred of the other painter was the problem holding him back from finishing the work. Only after forgiving the other painter and repainting the face of Judas could he complete Jesus' face. This story shows how much of a stumbling block failure to forgive can be to our lives. Jesus forgave us so that we might forgive others and be released not only from our sin but also from the weight of bearing grudges.

Genealogy

A line of descent traced continuously from an ancestor.

Origin: from Greek genealogia, *from* genea, *meaning
'race or generation'.*

In recent years there has been a surge of interest in family trees. People have sought to trace back family lines and origins as far as they possibly can. This is a natural desire, since we all want to know where we came from and how we got here.

The two genealogies in the New Testament both trace the lineage of Jesus Christ: Matthew 1.1–17 and Luke 3.23–38. Matthew begins with Abraham and follows the line through David to Jesus through Joseph's family. Luke begins with Jesus and outlines the genealogy of Mary's family line through David and all the way back to the beginning with Adam.

It is interesting to note that Matthew refers to Joseph not as the father of Jesus, but as 'Joseph, the husband of Mary. Mary gave birth to Jesus, who is called the Messiah' (Mt. 1.16). The Bible is clear that God, not Joseph, was the father of Jesus.

Glory

Praise, worship and thanksgiving offered to God.

Origin: from the Latin gloria, *meaning 'great praise or honour'.*

In our world outstanding performers, in sports or the performing arts, can be worthy of glory for what they have achieved. Those who have won Olympic gold medals, for example, experience in the public arena a certain amount of glory. Yet when Jesus was born, a mere baby, the Bible records that the shepherds 'gave him glory'. The appearance of the angels, who in themselves 'reflected the glory of God', was enough to convince the shepherds that this baby Jesus was no ordinary baby. He was significant and worthy of glory and praise.

Christians believe that the reason humans were created was to 'glorify' God. Christians endeavour to live lives that 'do all for the glory of God' (1 Cor. 10.31). This is not an easy task and often Christians fall short of a God who is perfectly loving, powerful and glorious. It may seem that God was fairly self-righteous to create people to worship him, but he is a creative God and, as the author and originator of all life, is surely worthy of glory and praise.

Goodwill

Friendly or helpful feeling or attitude.

Christmas is often known as the 'season of goodwill' when we especially remember those in need. This originated from Victorian times when emphasis was placed on giving to the poor and remembering the less fortunate.

Some people criticize the apathetic attitudes of many people at Christmas, as they fail to give any recognition to those with less than themselves. Even in 1702 this was a concern, and *Poor Robin's Almanac* complained about aristocratic slackers at Christmas:

> *And fiddlers who used to get scraps*
> *Now cannot fill their hungry chaps;*
> *Yet some true English blood still lives,*
> *Who gifts to the poor at Christmas gives,*
> *And to their neighbours makes a feast,*
> *I wish their numbers would increase . . .*

There may still be some 'true English blood', with charities increasing their push for donations at Christmas and many people giving generously, but no doubt each of us could do with offering more goodwill to those around us during the festive season.

Handel

George Frideric Handel's *Messiah* is probably the most popular piece of Christmas music. Although the words focus on the resurrection, it is traditional to perform the *Messiah* oratorio during Advent, in the run-up to Christmas.

At the request of the Duke of Devonshire, Handel wrote the *Messiah* for the benefit of Irish charities. He wrote it in only 24 days and produced 256 pages of manuscript, primarily from the words of Charles Jennings' biblical 'Libretto'. In 1742 Handel conducted the first performance of the *Messiah* in Dublin with 36 musicians and 24 singers. It was an immediate success and a newspaper reported: 'The hall was crowded . . . the performance was superior to anything of the kind in the kingdom before . . . Words are wanting to express the exquisite delight it afforded the admiring crowd.'

The most well-known movement of this work is the 'Halleluiah Chorus', which concludes the second of the three parts. It is said that on the first hearing King George II became so excited that he rose to his feet, compelling the rest of the crowd also to stand. In many parts of the world it has been accepted practice ever since to stand during this section.

Handel was governor of the Foundling Hospital in London, which helped poor and orphaned children. He gave performances every year there until 1754, after which he presented the original score of the *Messiah* to the hospital. In 1784 there was a special performance of the *Messiah* in

Westminster Abbey with 253 players and 257 singers. In 1857 Queen Victoria attended a performance at the Crystal Palace with about 20,000 other people. By this time the orchestra contained 500 people and there were 2,000 singers. In 1910 the oratorio was performed with 5,000 singers at Crystal Palace.

Hanukkah

An eight-day Jewish festival of lights held in December,
commemorating the rededication of the Jewish temple in
Jerusalem in 165 BC after its desecration.

Origin: Hebrew, meaning 'consecration'.

Two hundred years before Jesus' birth, the Jewish people lived in Judea, part of Palestine ruled by the Syrian Antiochus IV. When the king plundered the treasures of the holiest Jewish shrine, the Jews retaliated. Under the leadership of the priest Mattathias and Judah of the Maccabees, the Jewish temple was retaken from the Syrians in 167 BC. The relighting of the 'menorah', the temple candelabra, was part of the rededication ceremony and although there was only a tiny supply of oil the candles burned for eight days, which was seen as a miracle. So Hanukkah celebrates two miracles, the end of the Syrian occupation and the miracle of the lights. The greatest triumph was the Jewish ability to thwart the Syrian attempt to eradicate their customs and identity. If Judaism had not survived as a belief, a way of life and a covenant with God, there would be no Nativity or Christmas, as Jesus was born a Jew.

Hanukkah is a time of gift-giving, a popular gift being 'Hanukkah gelt', chocolate coins covered with gold foil. One of the most visible aspects of the observance of Hanukkah is the lighting of nine candles, usually put in a prominent place such as the window of a house. It is from this practice that the celebration derived its second name, the 'Festival of Lights'. Coinciding with the Christmas season, it ensures that all Judeo-Christian societies will be well lit with various displays of symbolic light.

Herod

Ruled Judea from 40 BC until his death in 4 BC.

Herod was appointed by the Roman Senate to be King of Judea in 40 BC and by 37 BC he controlled most of current-day Israel and Palestine. He even called himself 'King of the Jews', and he was known by that title until his death. That was why he felt threatened when he heard that someone had been born who was also being called 'King of the Jews'.

Herod was ruthless and his palace was full of intrigue and tragedy. His paranoia was legendary. He executed his uncle, his mother-in-law, his wife Mariamme, two of his sons and a barber. His entire life was one of plotting and execution. After the birth of Jesus he ordered the slaughter of all boys under the age of two in Bethlehem, in an attempt to kill Jesus, the 'baby king'. This is known as the 'Slaughter of the Innocents' and is recorded in Matthew's Gospel. In medieval times this terrible event was remembered as 'Childermass' and celebrated on 28 December. Today it is more commonly referred to as Holy Innocents' Day.

Josephus, a Jewish historian, wrote a few years after Herod's death:

> *He was no king but the most cruel tyrant who ever ascended the throne. He murdered a vast number of people and the lot of those he left was so miserable that the dead might count themselves fortunate . . . within a few years the Jews suffered more misery through Herod than their forefathers had done.*

Herod was replaced by his son Herod Antipas (21 BC–AD 39), who ruled throughout the ministry of Jesus.

Holly and ivy

*Holly: an evergreen shrub with prickly dark green leaves, small
white flowers and red berries.*

*Ivy: a woody evergreen climbing plant, typically with shiny
five-pointed leaves.*

———————

No plants have a warmer association with Christmas than holly (*Ilex
aquifolium*) and ivy (*Hedera helix*). Such evergreens are used for
Christmas decorations because they still look fresh during the winter
months. The idea of using festive greens was not originally a Christian
practice, and they have been favourite winter decorations for thousands of
years. Before the birth of Christ pagans decorated their altars, temples
and sanctuaries for festivities. Evergreen plants that survived the winter
blast were thought to hold magical and mystical powers for promoting
rich harvests, personal health and fertile marriages. The ancient Romans
gave sprigs of holly as gifts to one another. Even after the Roman Empire
had become Christianized many people continued to decorate their
homes with winter greenery and the custom became part of the Christian
celebration of Christmas.

Christians also use holly because of the imagery that can be drawn from it in relation to Jesus, as can be seen in the carol 'The Holly and the Ivy':

The holly and the ivy,
when they are both full grown,
of all the trees that are in the wood,
the holly bears the crown.

The holly bears a berry,
As red as any blood.
And Mary bore sweet Jesus Christ,
To do poor sinners good.

The holly bears a prickle,
As sharp as any thorn.
And Mary bore sweet Jesus Christ
On Christmas Day in the morn.

The holly bears a bark,
As bitter as any gall.
And Mary bore sweet Jesus Christ,
For to redeem us all.

I

Immanuel

*All of this occurred to fulfil the Lord's message through his prophet: 'Look!
The virgin will conceive a child! She will give birth to a son, and they will
call him Immanuel, which means "God is with us".' (Mt. 1.22–3)*

Jesus was called Immanuel, which in Hebrew literally means 'God
with us'. It was prophesied that God himself would appear as
a human infant. More remarkable than a baby in a manger is the truth
that this promised baby is the omnipotent Creator of the heavens and the
earth. It took enormous humility and great sacrifice for Jesus to leave the
glory of heaven and come to live among us. To be Immanuel is the miracle
of Christmas.

Did you ever spend time as a child watching ants working and
scurrying around their anthill? It's intriguing to watch the tiny ants
struggle to move a twig, part of a leaf, or a piece of food across difficult
terrain, and then chop it up and drag it down their tunnels for storage
under the earth. We are so much more powerful and capable than ants.
It is so easy for a person to crush an ant inadvertently, just by walking. It
can seem that compared to an ant, we have almost God-like power.

Would you be willing to become an ant? Would you be willing to
empty yourself of your humanity and live as an ant, with all the danger,
profound limitations and vulnerability that would entail? It is unlikely
that this kind of life holds any appeal to us at all.

There is a vast gulf between human life and insect life. Just think, however, about the awesome gulf that exists between God and humanity. We are far below God's level. We are mortal, vulnerable to sickness and injury, limited in time, in space, in our capacities and our intelligence, and we live a life that is but a shadow of life.

This emphasizes the incredible miracle of Jesus' birth — that he was willing to take upon himself physical flesh and live out a human life with all its limitations. Yet, it happened. He loved us so much that he became one of us. Not only that, but we can celebrate 'Immanuel' every Christmas. Although physically he is no longer amongst us, he promised that by the Holy Spirit we could know him and experience his love, joy and peace.

Christmas can be a time when loneliness is most keenly felt, when the pain of broken relationships and families is most acute. The good news is that we are not alone. If we could condense all the truths of Christmas into just three words, these would be 'God with us'.

*I*ncarnation

The embodiment of God the Son in human flesh
as Jesus Christ.

Origin: from Latin incarnare, *meaning 'make flesh'.*

In 1995 the singer Joan Osborne wrote and sang a popular song, 'One of Us', which asked the question, 'What if God were one of us?' A plea was made in this song, seeking to know why we exist. Where is God in all of this life, and what if he lived my life? The answer, of course, is that he did become one of us. That is what the incarnation is all about. Jesus 'is the visible image of the invisible God' (Col. 1.15).

John Howard Griffin was a white man who believed he could never understand the plight of African-Americans unless he became like one of them. In 1959 he darkened his skin with medication, sun lamps and stains and then travelled throughout America. His book, *Black Like Me*, helped white people to understand better the discrimination faced daily by people of colour. Jesus Christ became like us. The incarnation is evidence that God understands us. 'He was despised and rejected – a man of sorrows, acquainted with deepest grief' (Isa. 53.3).

The incarnation is the reason we celebrate Christmas. This is when God 'took flesh' in the human body of Jesus. The humble birth of Jesus was never intended to be a facade to conceal the reality that God was being born into the world. We cannot begin to comprehend why Jesus, who was infinitely rich, would empty himself, embrace a human nature and enter a world which he knew would reject and kill him.

Innkeeper

The innkeeper in Bethlehem was faced with a dilemma: a man with a pregnant wife and his inn fully booked. He turned Mary and Joseph away saying that he had no room for them. As far as we know he didn't even call for anyone to help a young mother about to give birth. Mary 'gave birth to her first child, a son. She wrapped him snugly in strips of cloth and laid him in a manger, because there was no lodging available for them' (Lk. 2.7).

Mary was vulnerable and alone. There were no midwives, no one came to help her. The Bible doesn't say whether Joseph was there. Under normal circumstances, custom would not have permitted his presence, and if he was typical of first-time fathers he would have been of little assistance anyway! Such circumstances for a birth in first-century Jewish culture were extremely unusual. Yet that is what happened. Mary did it herself. There was no basket for the newly born baby Jesus, so Mary had to lay him in an animal feeding trough.

The innkeeper turned away a young mother about to give birth and missed the first Christmas.

Jesse tree

A decorated tree put up during Advent, tracing the line of the Messiah in the Old Testament.

―――――――――

There was an old custom in Europe and early America whereby symbolic ornaments were hung on a tree during the Advent period leading up to Christmas. These decorations represented Old Testament events from the creation right up to the birth of Jesus, in particular the prophecies that foretold the coming Messiah. The Jesse tree was decorated each day or week of Advent, traditionally with ornaments handmade by children and their parents. Its name comes from Isaiah 11.1, 'Out of the stump of the line of Jesse (David's father) will grow a shoot – yes, a new branch bearing fruit from the old root'. This prophetic imagery, written centuries before Jesus, speaks of the Messiah who would come bringing hope to Israel from the lineage of David.

There is evidence for the concept of a Jesse tree from as early as the twelfth century, in the remains of stained-glass windows. Such trees are one of the most common glass designs found from this era, and they remained popular until the sixteenth century. In the last half-century they have risen in popularity again, as a means of rediscovering the historical message of Christmas. There are now many guidelines around for making a Jesse tree, for example *Let's Make a Jesse Tree!* by Darcy James.

Jingle Bells

Jingle: light loose ringing sound such as that made by metal objects being shaken together.

The song 'Jingle Bells' by James Pierpont was first published in 1857 with the title 'The One Horse Open Sleigh'. Only later was the title changed to 'Jingle Bells', and it is a song we can't escape from when Christmas shopping.

James Pierpont led an interesting, if not controversial, life. He was born in New England in 1822 to John Pierpont. James ran away from home at the age of 14, boarded a ship called *The Shark*, and served as a deckhand in the Pacific. Eventually returning to land, he headed to California during the Gold Rush. He was living in Savannah when he wrote 'Jingle Bells' and went on to become a music professor at the Quitman Academy.

King Wenceslas

King of Bohemia, c. AD 907–29.

Origin: from Old Czech Veceslavu, *meaning*
'having greater glory'.

Wenceslas was one of the first Christian rulers of Bohemia, now
part of modern Czechoslovakia. He was born in 907 in the castle
of Stochov near Prague. The castle no longer stands, but there is still an
oak tree that was supposedly planted by Ludmila, his grandmother, when
Wenceslas was born. At first Ludmila raised him. Then, when he was
about 13 years old, his father died and Wenceslas succeeded him as duke.
Because he was too young to rule, his mother, Drahomira, became regent.
Drahomira was opposed to Christianity and used her new power to
persecute followers of the Christian faith. She refused to let Wenceslas see
Ludmila because she was afraid they would scheme to overthrow her.
Eventually Ludmila was murdered at Tetin Castle – strangled, it is said, at
Drahomira's command. After her death Ludmila was revered as a saint.

The loss of his grandmother did not stop Wenceslas from seizing
power. At the age of 18 he overthrew his mother's regency, just as she
had feared, and began to rule for himself. A stern but fair monarch, he
stopped the persecution of priests and tamed the rebellious nobility. He
was known for his kindness to the poor, as the famous carol 'Good King

Wenceslas' describes. He was especially charitable to children, helping young orphans and slaves.

Many of the Bohemian nobles resented Wenceslas's attempts to spread Christianity and were displeased when he swore allegiance to the King of Germany, Henry I. Wenceslas's most deadly enemy proved to be his own brother, Boleslav, who joined the nobles in plotting his brother's assassination. He invited Wenceslas to a religious festival and then attacked him on his way to mass. As the two were struggling, Boleslav's supporters jumped in and murdered Wenceslas. He was in his early twenties and had ruled Bohemia for five years. Today he is remembered as the patron saint of the Czech Republic. We associate Wenceslas with 26 December because, as the carol tells us, it was 'on the feast of Stephen' that the good king went gathering fuel for his poorer subjects. Strictly speaking, St Wenceslas Day is on 28 December, for he was killed on that day in 929.

The words to the carol 'Good King Wenceslas' were written by John Mason Neale and first published in 1853. It is an unusual carol because it has no reference to the Nativity, yet it conveys the 'Christmas spirit' and encourages generosity to the poor:

> *Therefore, Christian men, be sure*
> *Wealth or rank possessing,*
> *ye who now will bless the poor*
> *shall yourselves find blessing.*

Lights

A source of illumination.

Origin: from Germanic Licht, *meaning 'light, brightness'.*

Part of the reason why Christmas lights are important is that in the West it is the darkest time of the year. As the days get shorter, our busy lifestyles don't allow us to stop our activities when the sun goes down, so illumination is necessary. This is not, however, the full story.

Lights add an atmospheric and magical feel to Christmas, whether they are on a tree or in the streets. In the last decade, the types of outdoor Christmas lights have increased greatly. The advent of the light-up Santa has brought with it many impressive displays on houses throughout the UK. Neighbours have had competitions for the most exterior lights or the most exquisite designs.

In the Philippines, the appearance of bright, star-shaped lanterns along the road signals the start of the Christmas season. Filipinos celebrate the Christmas season well before people in other countries do. Usually these star-shaped lanterns, called *parol*, will show up as early as September, along with the many other symbols of the Philippine holidays. The lanterns come in many different shapes and sizes, although the star-shaped design remains the most common. Most Filipinos simply hang their lanterns on doors and windows, keeping the streets of the Philippines aglow with colourful designs for over three months.

Light is also very symbolic of the Christmas season. It represents hope when life seems very dark, and it brings a sense of newness, as when the sun shines through the clouds after a storm. It is also a description of who Jesus is. The Bible tells us that Jesus coming to earth was actually 'the true light, who gives light to everyone . . . coming into the world' (Jn 1.9). Later in John's Gospel (8.12), Jesus says:

> *I am the light of the world. If you follow me, you won't have to walk in darkness, because you will have the light that leads to life.*

Jesus said that he is the light of the world. No matter how tough times are, no matter what indignities we must suffer in this life, some day those indignities will end and Jesus' triumph will be revealed. The sun never ceases to shine. Sometimes clouds get in our way and prevent us from observing it, yet we do not lose faith in the sun.

Living without spiritual light is far worse than living without physical light. Christmas is a time of gearing up for a new year when the days begin to get longer again, with new possibilities and new hope. It is also a time to look to the coming of Jesus into the world, the one who pierces through our mixed-up lives, in all their failings and darkness, with his glorious eye-opening light.

Live Aid

The most unprecedented musical event of the 1980s was Live Aid, which took place on 13 July 1985. Mushrooming into a 16-hour event and spanning two continents via satellite video (an enormous undertaking in 1985), the event featured artists from all over the world performing to raise money and awareness for the dire famine in Ethiopia, which claimed the lives of over 1.2 million people in 1984. It was spearheaded by Bob Geldof, a singer and songwriter who was inspired to 'do something' after seeing the devastating reports of the famine in Africa. In 1984, he organized Band Aid, a group of artists who recorded the song 'Do They Know It's Christmas'. The song became an instant global hit, selling over 50 million copies, with the proceeds going to help the needy people in Ethiopia. Band Aid's all-star line-up included Bananarama, Bob Geldof, Culture Club, David Bowie, Duran Duran, Eurythmics, Frankie Goes to Hollywood, Heaven 17, Human League, Kool and the Gang, Midge Ure, Paul McCartney, Paul Young, Phil Collins, Spandau Ballet, Status Quo, Sting, The Style Council, U2 and Wham. Geldof had hoped to raise £72,000 from the proceeds of the song, but it eventually raised over £8 million worldwide. Twenty years later, in 2004, Band Aid 20 released a remake of the song, hitting the Christmas number one slot once more. What started as a little compassion from Bob Geldof has led to something of a Christmas tradition.

Magi

The three wise men from the East who brought gifts to Jesus.

Origin: plural of magus, *from Old Persian meaning
'a member of a priestly caste of ancient Persia'.*

Most of the popular ideas about the Magi are misleading. The popular carol 'We Three Kings of Orient Are' is suspect, as there is no evidence that there really were three of them, only that they brought three kinds of gifts.

Matthew's Gospel, originally written in Greek, speaks of the Magi from the East visiting Jesus. The ancient Greek historian Herodotus records that the Magi were a priestly caste of the Medes. The Medes occupied the land east of Palestine and south of the Caspian Sea, which is modern-day Iran.

Why did these Magi become 'wise kings' when there is nothing to indicate this in the Gospels? It is most likely because of the reference to these visitors in the Old Testament: 'The western kings of Tarshish and other distant lands will bring him tribute. The eastern kings of Sheba and Seba will bring him gifts' (Ps. 72.10). Early Christians therefore assumed that the Magi were kings.

Over time, European monarchs cemented this belief in the kings by embracing the idea that royalty were the first visitors to Jesus. The

Renaissance world was dominated by secular and ecclesiastical nobles, which explains why artwork concerning the Nativity usually features exotic kings in rich, colourful robes.

Legend tells how Mary gave each king a band from Jesus' swaddling clothes. All three men were supposedly converted to Christianity and are said to have died for their faith in India. The story continues that their bodies were sent to Constantinople by the Empress Helena, mother of Constantine the Great. Their bodies were later moved to Milan and transported by the German Emperor Barbarossa to Cologne Cathedral, where there is a tomb today containing the relics.

Whatever their motives at the beginning of their journey, when the wise men saw Christ 'they bowed down and worshipped him' (Mt. 2.11). God gave the Magi insight and understanding to see that Christ was God in human form.

Magnificat

The song of the Virgin Mary used as a canticle, especially at Vespers or Evensong.

Origin: literally 'magnifies', from the first words of the song, which translate as 'my soul magnifies the Lord'.

Oh, how my soul praises the Lord.
How my spirit rejoices in God my Saviour!
For he took notice of his lowly servant girl,
and from now on all generations will call me blessed.
(Lk. 1:46-7)

———————————

The Magnificat, Mary's song of praise recorded in Luke, is one of the most recognizable passages in the Bible. This is the stirring song Mary sings as she is greeted by her cousin Elizabeth, and it flows without rehearsal or forethought from the heart of a believing and obedient young woman.

Mary certainly had a lot to talk over with Elizabeth. She had been told by an angel that she was to become pregnant, but not by her fiancé Joseph. What would be the implications? The Jewish law was quite explicit in condemning this kind of thing. Every Jewish girl knew of the promised Messiah, but such thoughts were not remotely part of her agenda. Why should she be the one to be the mother of the Messiah? And so Mary journeyed south to Jerusalem to visit Elizabeth and her husband Zechariah, a priest who himself had received an extraordinary angelic visitation.

In the song Mary worships God and thanks him for choosing her, a humble servant girl, to be the mother of Jesus. She glorifies God because of the great and awesome things he has done. In this we can see Mary's genuine humility. She realized she was lowly, yet she praised God for choosing her for a special mission.

Mary's words are beautiful, powerful and moving. It is no surprise that composers have put her words to music time and again. These musical versions of her song are called 'Magnificats'. Three well-known versions are by Monteverdi (from his 1610 *Vespers*), J.S. Bach and Mozart (from *Vesperae solennes de confessore*).

Manger

A long trough for feeding horses or cattle.

Origin: from Old French mangeure, *derivative of* mangier, *'to eat'.*

It is likely that the manger in which Jesus was laid was made of wood and shaped like an open basket, perhaps lined with a woollen blanket. It is not known if Mary had help delivering Jesus, but at the time it was usual for women from the community to give advice and assistance during childbirth. Custom would not have allowed Joseph to be present. As soon as babies were born they were washed and rubbed with salt. This acted as an antiseptic and prevented infection. The belief was also that babies should be wrapped tightly in 'swaddling bands', like bandages.

In the ancient world, as well as in primitive modern cultures, mangers were kept within the house. A small number of flock animals were housed not in exterior sheds, but inside the house in one of the ground-floor rooms. By being inside, the animals were protected from the elements and from theft. In addition their presence provided extra body heat for cool nights, access to milk for the daily meal and dung as a critical fuel source. Excavations in Israel have uncovered numerous installations within domestic structures which represent ancient mangers. Some are carved, but most are built from stone.

A popular children's song at Christmas is 'Away in a Manger', which in the first two verses paints a picture of the Nativity scene. The music was composed by William James Kirkpatrick (1838–1921), to words by an unknown American author.

> Away in a manger, no crib for a bed,
> the little Lord Jesus laid down his sweet head.
> The stars in the night sky looked down where he lay,
> the little Lord Jesus, asleep on the hay.
>
> The cattle are lowing, the baby awakes,
> But little Lord Jesus, no crying he makes;
> I love thee, Lord Jesus, look down from the sky
> And stay by my cradle till morning is nigh.
>
> Be near me, Lord Jesus, I ask thee to stay
> Close by me forever, and love me, I pray;
> Bless all the dear children in thy tender care,
> And fit us for heaven to live with thee there.

Melchior

Origin: derived from Semitic roots, meaning 'king city'.

Melchior, who was the King of Arabia, was considered to be the oldest of the wise men who visited Christ. Melchior's gift to the Christ child was gold. The most precious metal then known, gold was a symbol of royalty and kingship from the earliest times. By giving Christ gold, Melchior was acknowledging Christ's kingship and offering him the best he had.

Merry

Cheerful and lively, characterized by festivity.

*Origin: of Germanic origin, related to 'mirth', meaning
'amusement and laughter', from Old High German* murg,
meaning 'short-lived'.

'Merry Christmas!' It's written everywhere over the festive season. In the Germanic dialect from which the words originated, such a greeting would mean 'short-lived Christmas!' and that doesn't at first appear to be something many people would say to their friends. However, its connection to pleasure comes most likely from the notion of 'making time fly', and suddenly the greeting fits the Christmas season perfectly. After months of excitement and preparation, the Christmas celebrations are over before you know it.

Drinking alcohol was always part of the pagan winter festivals and despite the Christian adaptation of Christmas drinking and feasting remained a central part of the celebration. Today people do tend to drink more at Christmas and a favourite drink is traditional punch, normally a combination of spirits with orange juice, lemonade, wine and cider. During Stuart times the Puritans banned Christmas, largely due to their concern at the high alcohol consumption during the season. Yet Robert Herrick, a country vicar, eulogized the merriment of the festival, showing how important Christmas was to the population and how unpopular the ban was:

> *Come, bring with a noise,*
> *My merrie, merrie boyes,*
> *The Christmas log to the firing;*
> *While my good Dane, she*
> *Bids ye all be free;*
> *And drink to your hearts' desiring.*

The following adaptation of a famous carol highlights the problems of too much merriment at Christmas time:

On the twelfth day of Christmas, my true love gave to me:
12 gin and tonics,
11 tequila slammers,
10 double vodkas,
9 shots of whiskey,
8 pints of bitter,
7 rum and blacks,
6 Southern Comforts,
5 Snakebites and black,
4 stomach aches,
3 dodgy curries,
2 throwings up,
and a trip to casualty . . .

Messiah

The promised deliverer of the Jewish nation prophesied in the
Old Testament of the Bible.

Origin: from Hebrew masiah, *meaning 'anointed'.*

Jesus' Messiahship has been the core reason for the differences between Christians and Jews since the time of the early church. To Jews, whatever wonderful teacher and storyteller Jesus may have been, he was just a human, not the Son of God. In the Jewish view, Jesus cannot save souls; only God can. For Christians, the central tenet of their faith is the belief that Jesus is the Son of God, the Messiah. For Christians Jesus was God in the flesh, who came to earth to absorb the sins of humankind and to free from sin those who accepted who he was. This truth has inspired adoration in people throughout the centuries, Handel's oratorio the *Messiah* being one glorious expression of this worship.

Midnight Mass

The Christian Eucharist or Holy Communion
taken on Christmas Eve.

Origin: from the Latin messa, *meaning 'eucharistic service'.*
Literal meaning 'dismissal', from the concluding words of the
service, 'Ite, missa est', meaning 'Go, (the prayer) has been sent',
or 'Go, it is the dismissal'.

In many countries Midnight Mass is the distinctive Christmas service, a great and unique event. Midnight Mass was introduced in Rome in the early fifth century, in memory of the Last Supper. The first of the three masses traditionally celebrated on Christmas Day, it was first celebrated by the Pope towards midnight on Christmas Eve in the chapel of the

Santa Maria Maggiore Basilica in Rome, with just a small congregation. This chapel had been constructed in 440 by Pope Sixte III to house a crib scene replicating the one in Bethlehem, to aid worship to Jesus. Midnight Mass would culminate with the procession of the Christ child, in which a family would have the privilege of representing the Holy Family and parade through the chapel.

This mass was special due to the belief by some that the Messiah was born on the stroke of midnight, as expressed in the fourth-century Latin hymn '*Quando noctis medium*'. Solemn and impressive, with rich carols, times of reflection and joyful celebration, and candlelight sparkling in the dimly lit buildings, the service has traditionally captivated the hearts of those who participate.

In Spanish and Latin countries, legend tells that the only time a rooster ever crowed at midnight was at the time of Christ's birth. Midnight Mass is consequently referred to as the 'Mass of the Rooster' in these communities. The Polish Midnight Mass is called *Mass Pasterka* ('Mass of the Shepherds'), so named to commemorate the shepherds who visited the first Nativity scene. In some countries shepherds are specifically honoured at the service on Christmas Eve. In Switzerland it is said that if someone stops at nine public fountains and takes three sips from each on the way to Midnight Mass, they will find their future spouse waiting at the entrance to the church.

Mince pies

Small pie containing mincemeat, typically eaten at Christmas.

Origin: 'mince' from Latin minutia, *meaning 'smallness'. 'Pie' from Latin* pica, *meaning 'magpie', used because the various combinations of pie ingredients are compared to objects randomly collected by a magpie.*

The origins of mince pies can be traced far back into history. In the twelfth century European knights returning from crusades in the Holy Land brought back with them many Middle Eastern ways of cooking. Recipes of meat cooked with fruit and sweet spices were popular then, mixing sweet tastes with savoury. In Tudor times mince pies were still a mixture of meat and fruit. They were called 'shrid' pies because they were made by shredding the meat and suet (hard fat found around the kidneys of cows or sheep). Dried fruit would be added, along with cinnamon, cloves and nutmeg. These three spices were said to be symbolic of the three gifts given by the wise men to Jesus. The mixture was placed in an oblong tin and, being representative of Jesus' crib, the picture of a small baby often decorated the lid. These pies were much larger than the ones we are used to today.

One pie in 1770 is recorded as having among its ingredients a hare, a pheasant, a capon, two rabbits, two pigeons and two partridges, as well as eggs, pickled mushrooms and spices. Sometimes these 'crib' pies could weigh as much as 220lbs (99.8kg).

Jack Horner was steward to the Abbot of Glastonbury, and he had to take a pie to King Henry VII as a present from the Abbot. Under the crust were the title deeds of 12 manors, sent to the king in the hope that he would not pull down Glastonbury Abbey. It is said that King Henry actually received only 11 deeds. What happened to the missing deed? That remains a mystery, but a song has been written remembering Jack:

> *Little Jack Horner*
> *Sat in a corner,*
> *Eating a mincemeat pie.*
> *He stuck in his thumb,*

And pulled out a plum,
And said, 'What a good boy am I.'

As with many other Christmas traditions, Oliver Cromwell and the Puritans tried to ban mince pies. The ban was lifted when Charles II reinstated Christmas. During the nineteenth century the mince pie underwent a major change. The new pie was round, instead of the traditional oblong, and the meat was replaced with nuts, apples and raisins. The pie was therefore much sweeter and instead of being offered at the beginning of a meal was saved for the finale.

Mistletoe

Leather-leafed parasitic plant which grows on broadleaf trees and bears white berries in winter.

Origin: from the Old English mistletan, *meaning 'different or special twig'.*

In ancient times mistletoe was thought of as the plant of peace and friendship. If enemies met under a tree on which mistletoe grew, they would lay down their arms and call a truce for the rest of the day. If friends met beneath a tree bearing mistletoe, they would consider their friendship to be blessed with good fortune.

Kissing under the mistletoe is a distinctly British tradition. It is probably significant that the Celts and Scandinavians, two peoples for whom mistletoe was particularly special, dominated Britain in the past. In Scandinavia mistletoe has long been associated with Freyja, the goddess of love. The story goes that Freyja's son was killed with an arrow tipped with mistletoe and her tears turned to white berries. When he was brought back to life she kissed everyone who passed underneath the tree that was covered in mistletoe.

In the Middle Ages people were encouraged to gather 'holy boughs' of evergreens and make decorations to hang near the doors of their homes. The priest would then make rounds of the village, blessing the boughs and the homes displaying them. As visitors passed under the boughs they would be welcomed with a hug, an appropriate expression of Christian love. It is thought a chaste kiss was added to the custom later on, but it is unlikely that this was the origin of the romantic kiss under the mistletoe.

There are many superstitions still associated with mistletoe. Apparently no girl can refuse a kiss from a man under the mistletoe. But if a girl stands there and no one kisses her, then she will go a year without love.

An ancient name for mistletoe is 'the wood of the holy cross'. According to legend, mistletoe wood was used to make the cross on which Christ died. After the execution the mistletoe shrivelled up with shame, changing its form from a tree to a creeper. Mistletoe was never taken into a church, and some churches still refuse to have it as part of evergreen decorations at any time.

Mulled wine

Warm wine with sugar and spices added to it.

Mulled wines have a long history. In medieval times they were called 'ypocras' or 'hipocris', named after the physician Hippocrates. They were thought to be very healthy, and indeed, with wine at the time being far more sanitary than water, these heated drinks in all likelihood did keep people healthy through the cold winters.

Moving forward to the 1500s, cookbooks listed methods of mulling 'Clarrey', or Bordeaux. Recipes involved honey, cinnamon, cardamon, galingale and French wine. Mulled wine was a favourite in Victorian England, and negus – a type of mulled wine – was even served to children at their birthday parties.

There are many varieties of mulled wine and there are different styles in every part of the world, some favouring white wine, others red. Some add only a few spices, while others pour in oranges, cloves, 12 spices and more fruit for colour. 'Mull' is an Old English word for dust, so mulled wine may mean 'dusted with spices'. Spices, of course, are reminiscent of the gifts given to the Christ child by the wise men.

Many liquids can be mulled – mead, cider and beer as well as wine. Mulled wine is a traditional favourite in cooler locations, and goes well with the various celebrations that come around at the end of the year. Glühwein ('glow wine') is similar to mulled wine and is a popular Christmas drink in Austria, Switzerland and Germany. It contains red wine, fruit, cloves and cinnamon and is served hot by street vendors at Christmas fairs.

Mummers' play

Traditional English folk play of a type often associated with Christmas and popular in the eighteenth and early nineteenth centuries.

Origin: 'mummer' from the Old French momeur, from momer, meaning 'act in a mime'.

Mumming originated from the Saturnalia festivities of ancient Rome, which arrived in Britain when the Romans occupied the country. In the Middle Ages mummers' plays were a popular tradition all over Europe, passed down orally from generation to generation. Costumes were very unusual: some mummers who entertained King Edward III of England in 1347 dressed up as rabbits.

The central figure of mummers' plays is often St George and the main story generally involves a fight and the arrival of a doctor to bring the slain back to life. Mock swords are often used, and there is a connection with morris dancing, in which the dancers use sticks in mock fights. It is uncertain why St George came to be the central figure of these Christmas plays, but the connection may have come from the medieval pageants of many English towns.

Old mumming plays almost died out at the beginning of the twentieth century, because many of the men who would have learnt the old plays were killed at war. Today, however, some old plays have been revived. Plays are performed in Gloucester on Boxing Day, for example, and in Moulton in Northamptonshire, Marshfield in Bristol and Crookham in Hampshire. In the US the Philadelphia Mummers' Parade takes place on New Year's Day. The parade, which started over 100 years ago, has grown into a huge procession of floats, mumming groups, marching bands and other entertainments.

Mystery play

A popular medieval play based on biblical stories,
performed by local craft guilds.

Origin: from Latin ministerium, *meaning 'trade, ministry,*
craft'. Also influenced by medieval Latin mysterium, *meaning*
'divinely revealed religious truth or rite'.

———————————

The two senses of the title 'mystery' formed a common pun in Tudor theatre, where craftsmen acted out religious stories, often in a humorous manner. Mysteries began as religious processions or pageants performed by groups of merchants or craftsmen who formed associations called 'guilds', meaning 'payment' or 'offering'. Each town's guild had a beautifully decorated cart, which formed part of a procession. For example, the goldsmiths would pay for the float showing the arrival of the Magi to visit Jesus. The existence of pageant wagons is first recorded in York from 1376.

Gradually words were added and little plays were performed. Mystery plays tended to involve much slapstick comedy, favourite characters being three shepherds called Hanken, Harvey and Tudde. These characters were not very bright and spent their time arguing about what the angel of the Lord had said to them. Herod was the villain and everyone loved to hate him. He would growl, snort, scream and run around the audience. Dummies were used with copious amounts of fake blood to re-enact the Massacre of the Innocents.

Mystery plays were often performed in groups of plays called 'cycles'. The most famous ones in England were the Chester, Coventry, York and Wakefield Cycles. The York Cycle attracted great crowds and was made up of 48 plays which illustrated the Christian history of the world from the Creation to the Last Judgement. The performance started at 4.30 a.m. and lasted all day. The solitary surviving manuscript of the York plays, dating from around 1463–77, is kept at the British Library. In France there were mystery cycles that had 500 speaking parts, 60,000 lines and took 40 days to complete.

In 1568 the plays were banned by the Puritans. It was not until 1951 that they were staged once again, as part of the Festival of Britain.

Noel

Christmas, especially as a refrain in carols and on Christmas cards.

Origin: French, based on Latin nasci, *meaning 'be born', and* natalis, *meaning 'birthday'. Related words are found in many languages around the world:* Nowell *in Old English,* Natal *in Spanish,* Natale *in Italian,* Nadal *in Provencal.*

Noels can be seen at their earliest in fifth-century manuscripts and are songs or poems of feasting and rejoicing. The famous song 'The First Noel' is probably remembered for its repetition – the carol contains the word 'noel' 29 times. It first appeared in print in England in a collection by William Sandys in 1833. Most people think it is from sixteenth- or seventeenth-century France; others (apparently struck by the three wise men's politeness to a foreigner) contend that it couldn't possibly be French and instead has English roots.

Another carol with 'Noel' in its title is *'Cantique de Noel'* ('O Holy Night'), heralded as one of the most beautiful carols with its rich music and superb lyrics. This carol was written by Adolphe Charles Adam (1803–56), the French composer best known for his ballet *Giselle*. At the time the carol was attacked by church authorities as having a 'total absence of the spirit of religion'. This was more to do with the reputation of the composer than the contents of the song, however, and from the turn of the century it was recognized as beautifully capturing the joy of Christmas.

Nuts

A hard-shelled, one-seeded fruit.

An archaeological dig in Israel found evidence showing that nuts formed a major part of people's diet thousands of years ago. Seven varieties of nut, along with stone tools to crack them open, were found buried deep in a bog. Historians also say that almonds, mentioned in the Old Testament of the Bible, were among the earliest cultivated foods. The famous Arabian marzipan, a sweet paste candy made from ground almonds, was brought back by the Crusaders returning from the Holy Lands in the eleventh and thirteenth centuries and still remains popular today. The increase in vegetarianism in recent decades has made nut roast a popular alternative to turkey at Christmas.

Nuts, like fruit, were the original Christmas tree decorations. Nutcrackers dressed as soldiers were popular Christmas decorations after Tchaikovsky's ballet became famous in the 1890s. *The Nutcracker* tells the story of a little girl named Clara who, at her family's annual Christmas Eve party, is given a doll, a prince, by her beloved godfather Drosselmeier. The doll is made from a nutcracker and Clara loves it so much that after everyone has gone to bed she sneaks back down to the Christmas tree to look at it. She falls asleep and begins to dream. In her dream she finds her prince, the Nutcracker, who comes to save her from an army of mice and their king, who tries to kidnap her. The Mouse King nearly defeats the Nutcracker, but at the last moment Clara throws her shoe at the Mouse King and that is the end of him. The Nutcracker Prince then leads Clara off to visit his palace. On the way they pass first through the magical land of the Snow Queen and her Snowflakes, and then the Land of Sweets, where they are met by the Sugar Plum Fairy, who stages a series of dances for them, ending with the Waltz of the Flowers. But all wonderful dreams must end, and Clara awakens under her Christmas tree on Christmas morning surrounded by friends and family.

People have often said that nuts represent the fact that nothing in life comes without work. A proverb says, 'God gives us nuts but we have to break them ourselves.'

Pantomime

*Theatrical entertainment involving music, topical jokes and
slapstick comedy. Usually produced around Christmas.*

Origin: from Greek pantomimos, panto *meaning 'all kinds',
and* mimos *meaning 'mime'.*

People have always used the 'language of gestures', not only to
communicate but also to entertain. During the Roman Saturnalia
festivities people enjoyed silent mime performances, and the reign of
Augustus Caesar Pylades and Bathyllus brought both serious and comic
pantomimes to great perfection. These men opened a theatre in
partnership and, while Pylades presented solemn and pathetic subjects,
Bathyllus was more humorous and animated. Their performances were so
brilliant and astounding that people went wild with enthusiasm.

Modern-day pantomime draws its origins from aspects of *Commedia
dell'arte*, Italian theatre which was itself descended from the distant
Roman tradition of dumbshows performed by a single masked dancer
called Pantomimus. One of the main characters was Arlecchino, who in
Victorian Britain became Harlequin, a favourite pantomime character.

Something similar to pantomime was seen in eighteenth-century
England, but it was during the Victorian era that this entertainment
flourished. Pantomime was then a sort of variety show and even though

there was often an unbelievable story, it was enjoyed because of the jugglers, acrobats, comedians and songs.

Many popular pantomimes today are based on ancient stories. *Babes in the Wood*, for example, is over 500 years old and derives from a popular poem called 'The Children in the Wood'. *Puss in Boots* and *Sleeping Beauty* are over 450 years old. In 1717 the *Arabian Nights* stories were translated into English and many of these tales were made into pantomimes, including *Aladdin* and *Sinbad the Sailor*. We have the Victorians to thank for stories such as *Dick Whittington* and *Robin Hood*.

One of the most popular characters in modern-day pantomimes is Widow Twankey, a classic 'dame' and a role usually played by men. The character was originally Aladdin's mother, the Widow Ching Mustapha, but by 1870 she had adopted the name of Twankey, taken from a type of tea called *twankei* brought from China to England in the nineteenth century. The principal boy in pantomimes is always played by a girl and the part was first introduced in the 1880s by Augustus Harris, the manager of London's Drury Lane Theatre.

Peace

Freedom from disturbance, tranquillity.

Origin: from the Latin pax, *meaning 'peace'.*

And he will be called: Wonderful Counsellor, Mighty God, Everlasting Father, Prince of Peace. (Isa. 9.6)

At Christmas the word 'peace' will sound from billions of lips: in churches, on greetings cards, at the office, in the streets and in homes. World leaders will invoke both God and peace in the same breath. But the reality is that there is no peace. We have war on terrorism, war on famine, war between Jews and Arabs (in Bethlehem, of all places), drug wars, cyber wars, virtual wars, even war for the Christmas number one slot in the music charts. It doesn't seem to be a very peaceful time of year.

The Bible states that after the angel had appeared to the shepherds, 'Suddenly, the angel was joined by a vast host of others . . . praising God and saying, "Glory to God in highest heaven, and peace on earth to those with whom God is pleased"' (Lk. 2.13–14). So where is this much talked about 'peace on earth'? Since that night we have had very little political or military peace in the world. In spite of all the political deliberations and summits, peace on earth remains a distant dream. Did the angels sing the wrong word? Why did they sing about peace if there was to be no lasting peace in the world?

The answer is that they were primarily singing about peace with God. God is not happy with us because we have turned our backs on him and ignored him. That means that we are at war with God. You might think that's a bit strong, but even passively ignoring him, by living in his world as if he didn't exist, is hurtful to God. We may nod in his direction occasionally, but that doesn't make us friends with him. We say, 'I don't need you, thanks very much. I can run my own life, if that's all right with you!'

Yet the angel brought good news to the shepherds at Christmas – good news that remains just as life-changing today and allows us to have peace with God. The angels were also proclaiming the blessing of peace between the people of the earth. Christmas celebrates the birth of a man whose life and teaching shows us how we can bring peace to a fractured world. Knowing peace with God, we then work as peacemakers. God also encourages us to hold to the hope that one day all things will be made new, and truly we will have lasting peace.

Poinsettia

A small shrub with large showy scarlet bracts surrounding the
small yellow flowers — Euphorbia pulchermia.

Origin: named after the American diplomat and botanist
Joel Roberts Poinsett (1779–1851).

The Aztec people in Mexico were cultivating this colourful red and green plant long before it became a symbol of Christmas. In addition to admiring its beauty, the indigenous people of Mexico used the poinsettia both practically and spiritually. It was called *cuetlaxochitl* by the Aztec, meaning 'mortal flower that perishes and withers like all that is pure', and it represented purity and also the need for blood sacrifices. A dye was made from the plant's red bracts that was then used in religious ceremonies to represent blood. The plant was also used medically to treat skin infections and to fight fevers.

During the seventeenth century Franciscan priests near Mexico City were attracted to the poinsettia's winter bloom, and they used the flower for their Nativity processions. The poinsettia had reminded the Aztec of human blood sacrifices, but here it came to represent the sacrificial blood of Christ to Christians.

The plant owes its name to the first US ambassador to Mexico, Joel Roberts Poinsett. On a visit to Mexico in 1825 Poinsett saw the flower being used as a Christmas decoration, being known as 'the flower of the Holy Night'. He had a love for botany and sent some of these flowers back to his friends in America. This is where the poinsettias we see today come from, although they have been bred and developed for indoor decoration fit for the Christmas season. While red is still the most popular colour, they are now available in cream, yellow, peach and pink.

Port

A sweet dark red (occasionally brown or white) fortified wine, originally from Portugal.

Origin: shortened form of Oporto, a port in Portugal from which the wine was shipped.

In 1698 Britain declared war on France, and the subsequent blockade of French ports resulted in a shortage of wine for the British. British wine merchants approached the Portuguese, with whom the British had a good relationship. Unfortunately, the Portuguese wines were not of such a high quality as the French wines, and so the British decided to oversee production of the product themselves and British merchants added a bucket or two of brandy to 'stabilize' the wine on its journey back to Britain.

At first this technique did not meet with much appreciation, but when someone came up with the bright idea of adding the brandy before fermentation had finished (thus retaining the full and sweet flavour of the wine), port, as we know it today was born. Similar wines are now made in several other countries, notably Australia and the US.

Port wine is typically thicker, richer, sweeter and of a higher alcohol content than most other wines – roughly 20 per cent. It has been fortified with the addition of brandy, the effect of which is to kill the yeast in the part-fermented wine, thus producing a rich, strong, sweet flavour.

A toast often accompanies the drinking of port. The custom of drinking to 'health' is thought to be derived from the sixth century BC, when the Greeks toasted to the health of their friends for a highly practical reason – to assure them that the wine they were about to drink was not poisoned. To spike wine with poison had become an all too common means of dealing with social problems: disposing of an enemy, silencing the competition, preventing a messy divorce, and so on. It became a symbol of friendship for the host to pour wine from a common pitcher, drink it before his guests, and then raise his glass to his friends to encourage them to do likewise. The English term 'toast' can be traced to the seventeenth century and had reference at first to the custom of drinking to the ladies. In Stuart times it was the practice to put a piece of toast in the wine cup, in the belief that it improved the flavour of the wine. By then, drinking to health was a serious business. During Christmas 1643 the members of the Middle Temple drank to the health of the Princess Elizabeth by standing up one after another, pledging allegiance to her and swearing to die in her service.

Presents

A thing given to someone as a gift.

Origin: from Old French phrase mettre une chose en present a qualqu'un, *meaning 'put a thing into the presence of someone'.*

_____

Exchanging presents at Christmas is an important part of the festivities and no tree seems complete without colourfully wrapped presents sitting underneath it. It was Queen Victoria's husband Prince Albert who brought with him to England the German tradition of placing presents under the tree.

One of the earliest known customs of giving presents around the time of the winter solstice was during the Roman festival of the Kalends, which occurred on the first day of January. Such gifts were known as *strenae*. High-ranking officials of the Roman administration were expected to present gifts to their Emperor during the Kalends. In fact, Caligula went to the extent of declaring an edict that obliged them to do so. He would stand impatiently at the front door of his palace waiting for them to arrive.

The incorporation of presents into the Christmas tradition may also be a reflection of the three wise men giving gold, frankincense and myrrh to Christ. It does seem odd, however, that to celebrate the birthday of Christ we exchange gifts with each other. Just imagine if that happened on *your* birthday!

It seems more likely that we give gifts today simply because we want to. Psychologists have concluded that exchanging gifts is a critical way for societies to strengthen ties and define relationships. It is a fundamental form of social interaction.

Prophecy

An inspired message concerning the will of God,
often regarding future events.

Origin: from Greek prophetia, *meaning 'gift of interpreting*
the will of the gods'; originally from pro, *meaning 'before',*
and phetes, *meaning 'speaker'.*

———————

One very important component of a Christmas carol service is the reading of some of the prophecies concerning the coming Messiah. There are 322 messianic prophecies in the Old Testament, and they prepared the way for Jesus so that the Jews and later the Gentiles might believe in him as their Messiah and Saviour. They show God's control over the future and give us confident hope that all that God has promised will come to pass. They give us reason to trust in the Bible as being inspired by God.

The New Testament lists 52 prophecies being fulfilled in Christ's birth, for instance that he would be a descendant of King David (Isa. 11.1–5; Mt. 1.1, 6), and that he would be born in Bethlehem (Mic. 5.2; Mt. 2.1).

Jesus himself could not have controlled how these prophecies were fulfilled. No one can control the circumstances of their own birth, who their ancestors are and where they are born. Jesus could not control the actions of others in betraying him, putting him to death and laying his body in the unused tomb of a wealthy man. Yet the prophets had written these remarkable details in advance, up to 1,000 years earlier. King David prophesied details of Christ's death by crucifixion hundreds of years before the practice of crucifixion became common as a method of execution. Christians believe that many prophecies regarding Jesus Christ are yet to be fulfilled and will not be fulfilled until he returns to earth again.

Queen's speech

Queen: the female ruler of an independent state.

Speech: a formal address delivered to an audience.

Since the 1930s, a speech broadcast by the monarch on Christmas Day has become a familiar tradition in the UK. King George V started the Christmas message in 1932 with the development of new radio technology. That year had seen the beginning of the BBC's new service which sent radio programmes around the British Empire. Today this is known as the World Service. The king's message, written by the author Rudyard Kipling, was sent from a study in Sandringham House in Norfolk. A thick cloth covered the desk to mask the sound of rustling paper. The king famously said, 'I speak now from my home and from my heart to you all; to men and women so cut off by the snows, the desert, or the sea, that only voices out of the air can reach them.'

George V continued to broadcast at Christmas until his death in 1935. Edward VIII never delivered a Christmas broadcast, as his reign came to an end with his abdication before Christmas 1936. In 1937 George VI made it clear that he did not want to carry on the broadcast, as he felt it to be irretrievably linked to his father in the minds of the people. In 1939, however, with war having been declared some three months earlier and with unease being felt throughout the country and empire, the king decided to speak out to his people. Dressed in the uniform of the

Admiral of the Fleet, he sat in front of two microphones on a table at Sandringham. It was to be a landmark speech which had a profound effect on the listening public.

> *A new year is at hand. We cannot tell what it will bring. If it brings peace, how thankful we shall be. If it brings continued struggle we shall remain undaunted. In the meantime I feel that we may all find a message of encouragement in the lines which, in my closing words, I should like to say to you: I said to the man who stood at the Gate of the Year, 'Give me a light that I may tread safely into the unknown.' And he replied, 'Go out into the darkness, and put your hand into the Hand of God. That shall be better than light, and safer than a known way.'*

After George VI's death in 1952, his eldest daughter became Queen Elizabeth II and that year she broadcast her first Christmas message. She spoke of carrying on the tradition passed on to her by the late king.

> *Each Christmas, at this time, my beloved Father broadcast a message to his people in all parts of the world . . . My father and my grandfather before him worked hard all their lives to unite our peoples ever more closely. I shall strive to carry on their work.*

In 1953 the queen spoke from Auckland, New Zealand, the first and only time that the Christmas broadcast has been recorded outside the UK. In 1957, the twenty-fifth anniversary of the first Christmas broadcast, the queen's speech was televised from the Long Library at Sandringham.

The queen has given a Christmas broadcast in every year of her reign, with the exception of 1969. That year the film *Royal Family* had been shown by the BBC and it was decided not to do a special broadcast. The queen released a written message to newspapers instead, but the palace received many letters from people upset that there had been no Christmas broadcast. The television audience for the previous year had been estimated at over 23 million in the UK alone.

Whatever the current political, economic or social situation of the country or commonwealth, all three monarchs have always closed their message in the same way: by offering all their listeners and viewers the very best of wishes for a happy Christmas.

Reindeer

*A deer with large branching antlers, native to the northern
tundra and subarctic and domesticated in parts of Eurasia.*

R ock paintings by primitive peoples featuring reindeer are widespread,
as are discoveries of tools made from reindeer horn. The only
surviving civilization to live off reindeer is found in Lapland, the
northern part of Norway, Sweden and Finland. There are only a few
thousand Lapps, but they own herds of many thousands of reindeer.
From them the Lapps obtain meat, milk, hair for weaving, hides to make
tents and clothing, and horn for tools.

Reindeer have come to be associated with Christmas as the animals that
pull Santa's sleigh, and this is why Santa is said to live in Lapland. This
tradition came from stories of the Norse god Woden, who rode through
the sky with reindeer and 42 huntsmen. Although reindeer are the only
species of deer of which both sexes have antlers, the male reindeer shed
their antlers over the winter season. Therefore, according to the many
pictures depicting Santa's reindeer, every single one of them has to be a girl.

The famous poem 'Twas the Night Before Christmas' sealed the image
of Santa Claus, his reindeer and the magical flying sleigh loaded with
sacks of presents.

'Twas the night before Christmas, when all through the house
Not a creature was stirring, not even a mouse;
The stockings were hung by the chimney with care,
In hopes that St. Nicholas soon would be there;

The children were nestled all snug in their beds,
While visions of sugar-plums danced in their heads;
And mamma in her 'kerchief, and I in my cap,
Had just settled down for a long winter's nap,

When out on the lawn there arose such a clatter,
I sprang from the bed to see what was the matter.
Away to the window I flew like a flash,
Tore open the shutters and threw up the sash.

The moon on the breast of the new-fallen snow
Gave the lustre of midday to objects below,
When, what to my wondering eyes should appear,
But a miniature sleigh, and eight tiny reindeer,

With a little old driver, so lively and quick,
I knew in a moment it must be St Nick.
More rapid than eagles his coursers they came,
And he whistled, and shouted, and called them by name;

'Now, DASHER! now, DANCER! now, PRANCER and VIXEN!
On, COMET! on CUPID! on, DONNER and BLITZEN!
To the top of the porch! to the top of the wall!
Now dash away! dash away! dash away all!'

(Traditionally believed to be written by Clement Clarke
Moore (1779–1863), though some say the true author is
Major Henry Livingston Jr)

Robin

A small European songbird of the thrush family with a red breast and brown back and wings.

———————

It is hard to imagine Christmas without robins. Everywhere you look there are images of robins on cards, wrapping paper, cake decorations and crackers. But why is the robin so popular at Christmas? The answer lies in its red breast. When early Christmas cards were produced in the mid-eighteenth century, postmen wearing bright red coats delivered them. These postmen became known as 'robins' or 'redbreasts', and so the bird on the Christmas card was representing the postman who delivered it. In 1861, the postmen's uniform was changed to a more practical blue, but red has remained the traditional colour of the Royal Mail, reflected in its vans and letterboxes.

The legend of how the robin got its red breast is a story that has been told to children over the years.

The Legend of Robin Redbreast

On that first Christmas, it is said; the night was wrapped in a bitter chill. The small fire in the stable was nearly out, and the Mother Mary worried that her baby would be cold. She turned to the animals about her and asked them for help. 'Could you blow on the embers,' she asked the ox, 'so the fire might continue to keep my son warm?' But the ox lay sound asleep on the stable floor and did not hear her. Next, Mary asked the donkey to breathe life back into the fire, but the sleeping donkey did not hear Mary either. Nor did the horse or sheep. She wondered what to do. Suddenly, Mary heard a fluttering of little wings. Looking up, she saw a plain, brown-coloured little robin fly into the stall. This robin had heard Mary calling to the animals and had come to help her himself. He went over to the dying fire and flapped his wings hard. His wings were like little bellows, huffing and puffing air onto the embers, until they glowed bright red again. He continued to fan the fire, singing all the while, until the ashes began to kindle. With his beak, the robin picked up some fresh, dry sticks and tossed them into the fire. As he did, a flame suddenly burst forth and burned the little bird's breast a bright red. But the robin simply continued to fan the fire until it crackled brightly and warmed the entire stable. The Baby Jesus slept happily. Mary thanked and praised the robin for all he had done. She looked tenderly at his red breast, burned by the flame, and said, 'From now on, let your red breast be a blessed reminder of your noble deed. You will be known throughout the universe as the messenger of the Christ child, the true herald of Christmas. You are destined to travel the world telling the advent of the Saviour of mankind, and you will be part of the message of Christmas until the end of time and will always be known as the Christmas Robin.'

(Henry Livingston Jr, 1748–1828)

Rose

A prickly bush or shrub that typically bears red, pink, yellow or white fragrant flowers, native to north temperate regions and widely grown as an ornamental.

Christmas Rose: a stylized representation of a rose in heraldry or decoration.

Part of the colour in the celebration of the festive season is the blooming of Christmas roses. While a variety of plants over time have come to be called 'Christmas rose', they all are steeped in a legend that dates back to the last century.

'The Legend of the Christmas Rose' by Selma Lagerlöf was first published in 1908 in Swedish as part of a collection of stories, published in English as 'The Girl from the Marsh Croft' in 1910. The story tells of a young girl named Madelon who wanted to worship the Christ child. Seeing the gold, frankincense and myrrh brought by others who were drawn to the humble birthplace, she despaired that she had no gift to bring, for Madelon was very poor.

In vain she searched the countryside for a flower that she might bring, but the winter had been cold and harsh and there were no flowers to be found. Saddened, the girl began to weep. As she stood there weeping, an angel passing saw her sorrow and, stooping, he brushed aside the snow at her feet. There sprang up on the spot a cluster of beautiful winter roses, waxen white with pink-tipped petals. 'Nor myrrh, nor frankincense, nor gold,' said the angel, 'is offering more meet for the Christ child than these pure Christmas roses.' Joyfully Madelon gathered the flowers and made her offering to the Christ child.

Through the seemingly simple tale of a miracle Lagerlöf explores some of the basic tenets of Christianity — not judging people, the belief that anybody can be redeemed, and the rejection of materialism.

The Cornish refer to the Christmas rose as 'the Virgin's mantle'. Nicholas Culpeper's legendary seventeenth-century herbal publication refers to the 'Christmas herb' or the 'Christmas flower'. It was regarded as a suitable treatment for depression. It was first referred to as the 'Christmas rose' in the eighteenth century because of its resemblance to the single wild rose.

Rosemary

An evergreen aromatic shrub of the mint family,
native to southern Europe, the leaves of which are used as a
culinary herb, in perfumery, and formerly as an emblem
of remembrance.

Origin: from Latin ros marinus, *from* ros *meaning 'dew',*
and marinus *meaning 'of the sea'. Also influenced by 'rose' and*
Mary, mother of Jesus.

———

Rosemary is a herb that has been used widely since 500 BC and was once believed to strengthen the brain and memory functions. In Ancient Greece students would braid rosemary into their hair to bring them success during exams.

There are many legends surrounding rosemary, one being that it was used to awaken the Sleeping Beauty. Perhaps the best known is one that states that the plant will never grow taller than the height of Christ and, if it outlives the 33 years of Jesus' life, it will grow outward rather than upward. Another legend claims that the flowers were originally white, only changing to blue when Mary, on the flight from Egypt, threw her blue cloak over a bush, thus changing its colour and bestowing upon the plant its now distinctive fragrance. A variation of this legend holds that when the Holy Family fled to Egypt, they stopped to rest on a hillside. There, in a small stream, Mary washed Christ's clothes, spreading the tiny garments on a fragrant bush to dry in the sun. For its humble service the plant was named 'rosemary' and God rewarded it with delicate blossoms of the same heavenly blue that Mary's robe was supposed to be.

To Thomas Moore (whose garden was lavishly planted with rosemary) and Shakespeare's Ophelia, the herb symbolized remembrance. It was cultivated in monastery gardens for medicine and food and, according to medieval legend, rosemary decorating the altar at Christmas would bring special blessings and protection against evil spirits. It was also used to garnish the boar's head at the Christmas feast. American colonists even used rosemary as a scent for soap.

Until the twentieth century, rosemary was a much sought-after Christmas evergreen. A gilded rosemary sprig, for example, was considered to be a treasured gift. The reason for its later loss in popularity is unknown, but it is slowly starting to regain its former favour. It is once again included in festive wreaths, and rosemary topiaries are sometimes used as small Christmas trees.

Rudolph the Red-Nosed Reindeer

In 1939 Montgomery Ward and Company assigned Robert L. May, an advertiser, the job of writing a Christmas animal story as part of a marketing effort. Inspired by the story of the ugly duckling and his own background (he was often taunted as a child for being shy and small), May decided his story would be about a young, outcast reindeer triumphing over adversity. Rejected names for this character were Rollo, which was considered too cheerful and carefree for a misfit, and Reginald, which was considered too British. Eventually May settled on Rudolph and decided the trait that caused the other reindeers to shun him would be a glowing red nose. May's boss was worried that a story featuring a red nose – an image associated with drinking and drunkards – was unsuitable for a Christmas tale. May responded by taking Denver Gillen, a friend from Montgomery Ward's art department, to the Lincoln Park Zoo to sketch some deer. Gillen's illustrations of a red-nosed reindeer overcame the hesitancy of May's bosses, and the Rudolph story was approved.

The story tells how, on one foggy Christmas Eve, Santa was worried that he would not be able to deliver gifts that night. Rudolph, the outcast, saved Christmas by leading the sleigh by the light of his red nose. Rudolph's message – that, given the opportunity, a liability can be turned into an asset – proved popular. The story was an instant success and Montgomery Ward sold 2,400,000 copies in 1939 alone.

The post-war demand for licensing the Rudolph character was huge, but since May had created the story as an employee of Montgomery Ward they held the copyright and he received no royalties. Deeply in debt from the medical bills resulting from his wife's terminal illness (she died about the time May created Rudolph), May persuaded Montgomery Ward's corporate president, Sewell Avery, to turn the copyright over to him in January 1947. With the rights to his creation in hand, May's financial security was assured. *Rudolph the Red-Nosed Reindeer* was reprinted commercially in 1947, when it sold 3,500,000 copies.

In 1949 Johnny Marks composed the famous song 'Rudolph the Red-Nosed Reindeer'. Gene Autry recorded it and its immense popularity (it sold 2 million copies) further ingrained Rudolph in the Christmas imaginations of American children. Since then the story has been translated into 25 languages and made into a television movie, narrated by Burl Ives, which has charmed audiences every year since 1964.

S

St Anastasia

St Anastasia's Day falls on 25 December. Nothing is really known about this saint except that she died in AD 304, but that has not stopped many from trying to fill in the blanks. Tradition states that Anastasia was the daughter of Praetextatus, a noble Roman, and that she married a pagan named Publius, who died an early death. As a widow Anastasia cared for Christians enduring persecution, and then was arrested herself. On a ship with other prisoners, she was miraculously saved from drowning. She had gone to Sirmium (an ancient Balkan centre of Christianity, now in Serbia) to visit the faithful of that place, but was beheaded on the island of Palmaria on 25 December 304.

Anastasia enjoys the distinction, unique in the Roman Catholic liturgy, of having a special commemoration in the second mass on Christmas Day. This mass was originally celebrated not in honour of the birth of Christ, but in commemoration of this martyr, and towards the end of the fifth century her name was inserted into the canon of the mass.

St Nicholas

*Origin: from the Greek name Nikolaos, meaning
'victory of the people'. From the Greek nike, meaning
'victory', and laos, meaning 'people'.*

Nicholas was born during the third century in Patara, a village in what is now Turkey. His wealthy parents, who raised him to be a devout Christian, died in an epidemic while Nicholas was still young. Obeying Jesus' words to 'sell what you own and give the money to the poor', Nicholas used his inheritance to assist the needy, the sick and the suffering. He dedicated his life to serving Christ and was made Bishop of Myra while still a young man. His activities and accomplishments make great stories.

One such story involves a man and his three daughters. The man was desperately poor and could barely afford to feed and shelter his girls. Worst of all, he could not afford to provide them with marriage dowries and feared they would be spinsters. St Nicholas heard of the daughters' situation and resolved to help them. Not wanting to humiliate their father, he went to the family's house at night and tossed through the window a bag of gold, enough to cover the first daughter's dowry. Soon afterwards, on another night, St Nicholas tossed a second bag of gold into the house. Curious about this nameless benefactor, the father hid at the window each night, waiting to see who came. One evening, as Nicholas returned with the third bag, the father caught him. He promised not to disclose St Nicholas' identity, but he did later tell others about his extraordinary generosity.

Nicholas is said to have performed miracles similar to those of Jesus while aboard a ship returning from a Holy Land pilgrimage. On this journey a mighty storm threatened to wreck the ship. Nicholas prayed calmly. The terrified sailors were amazed when the wind and waves suddenly lessened, sparing them all. In later centuries ship owners would paint three bags of gold on the side of their vessels to represent the three gifts Nicholas had given the daughters of the poor man.

As a result of his seafaring adventures, Nicholas was prized as the patron saint of sailors and merchants. After his death in AD 434, medieval

106

port cities desired his remains. In 1087 sailors from Bari stole what were supposed to be the saint's bones from a Turkish crypt and, bringing them back to Bari, built a church to St Nicholas. The Venetians also claim they have the real bones of the saint in the church of St Nicholas on the Lido near the city. Nicholas was so widely revered that more than 2,000 churches have been named after him, including 300 in Belgium, 34 in Rome, 23 in the Netherlands and more than 400 in England.

St Nicholas also became the patron saint of children due to his generosity and particular concern for the young. Children in Russia, parts of Belgium, the Netherlands and Germany receive their Christmas gifts on 6 December, which is the saint's feast day. The idea of Santa Claus grew out of the legends of St Nicholas' generosity to children.

St Stephen

Origin: from the Greek name Stephanos, which means 'crown'.

Little is known of Stephen's early life, except that he was Jewish, like Jesus, spoke Greek and was probably brought up in Alexandria. Stephen was called by the 12 disciples of Jesus to help spread the good news of Christianity.

The New Testament tells us that when Stephen was heard arguing for the Christian faith he was reported to the Sanhedrin, the highest court of the Jewish people. They accused him of speaking against Moses and God. Stephen attacked the members of the court, calling them 'stubborn'. Anger at Stephen's words resulted in the court ordering him to be taken outside and stoned to death. As he was dying, Stephen prayed for his murderers. We do not have an exact date for Stephen's martyrdom, but it was probably around AD 35. Historically a martyr (from Greek *martys*, meaning 'witness') was considered to be a person who died for their religious faith, typically by being tortured to death.

You might say he was the second person to die for the Christian faith, after Jesus, so his feast day comes on the second day of Christmas, 26 December, unless it is a Sunday, when it moves to the next available day.

The Eastern Orthodox Church celebrates St Stephen's day on 27 December. The carol 'Good King Wenceslas' is really a St Stephen's Day song, because of the words, 'Good King Wenceslas looked down on the feast of Stephen.'

In Ireland St Stephen's Day is a public holiday, characterized by the legend of the Wren Boys. An old Irish legend says that when the Sanhedrin first put Stephen in prison, he would have escaped were it not for the chirping of wrens. On 26 December wrens were stoned to death in Ireland and other parts of Britain as part of a ceremony called the 'Wren Massacre'. The wrens were then paraded around the houses by groups of boys who would knock on doors asking for money. The killing of a bird is no longer tolerated, but the door-to-door visits continue. Most people treat the Wren Boys to pudding. Any young people in the house are cajoled to go on out with the group until there is a decent assembly of young folk being followed by most of the children in the neighbourhood. They will end up in some neighbour's house and if someone produces a fiddle the party begins!

St Thomas Becket

The feast of St Thomas is held on 29 December, after Thomas Becket who died on that day. He was born in 1118 and entered the church as a young man. By the age of 36, due to his favour with the king, he had become Chancellor of England under King Henry II. In 1162 he was made Archbishop of Canterbury. Thomas was worldly and ambitious, impetuous and harsh. Yet there was in him an idealistic, devout and pure side that would show itself more as he matured. After Thomas became archbishop his relationship with the king broke down and when Henry demanded that the church give up certain traditional rights, Thomas, as head of the church, refused.

In July 1170 monarch and archbishop met in France and patched up an agreement, but without discussing the principal issues. When Thomas returned to England on 1 December, the people greeted him triumphantly. In the late afternoon of 29 December 1170 knights arrived at Canterbury Cathedral and demanded that Thomas give in to the king's request. When he refused, the knights stormed in and grabbed the archbishop. They tried to drag him from the sacred place so that they could deal with him outside, but this proved impossible and finally two of the knights wounded Thomas with their swords while another delivered a blow to his head which fractured his skull.

All Europe was shocked at this sacrilegious assassination. Miracles were soon reported at Thomas Becket's tomb. The Pope excommunicated King Henry, who retracted his anti-church legislation and did public penance. Thomas was canonized in 1173. He had made up for his early failings by reforming his ways, but most of all by sacrificing his life for the liberty of the church.

Santa Claus

Father Christmas.

The original Dutch settlers in America spelled St Nicholas 'Sinter Nikolaas', which gradually changed to 'Sinterklaas'. As more English colonists arrived, this became 'Santa Claus'. The German settlers to America in the nineteenth century brought their own Christmas traditions too, one of which was the 'Christkind', an angelic child sent by Jesus to bring gifts to good children. With time the Christkind became the merry gift-bringer, Kriss Kringle.

In the US the image of Santa Claus was fostered especially by Clement Clarke Moore, who is traditionally believed to have written 'An Account of a Visit from St Nicholas', more famously known as 'Twas the Night before Christmas'. The St Nicholas of the poem is a jolly, red-cheeked elf with twinkling eyes and merry dimples — quite unlike the solemn bishop of the eighth century.

This was further developed, and the Santa Claus we know today with the big white beard, red coat, hat and trousers, black boots and a beaming red-cheeked face was created by American commercial artist Haddon Sundblom. In 1931 Sundblom was commissioned by Coca-Cola to illustrate their Christmas advertising campaign. The Coca-Cola Santa Claus was so popular that it became the internationally accepted view of what Santa Claus looked like.

The tradition of Santa coming down the chimney has come from variations of the St Nicholas story in which he places the bags of gold for poor children down the chimney instead of through the window. Another story, which is much older, also explains it. During the winter solstice each German house would be decorated with fir boughs and other evergreens to welcome Hertha, the German pagan goddess of the home. A platform of stones like an altar was built on the hearth (our word comes from her name) and evergreens were burnt on it. Hertha was believed to come down through the smoke of the blazing branches, rewarding the good and punishing the bad.

Santa's biography was written in 1902. It was created by Frank Baum, creator of Dorothy, Toto and the Wizard of Oz. In *The Life and Adventures of Santa Claus* Baum describes his origin, although it has little to do with the origins of St Nicholas and is nearly all imagined. In this account Santa started as an abandoned baby who was rescued by a nymph called Necile. Necile named the baby 'Claus', which meant 'a little one' in the language of the nymphs. In Baum's story Santa invented as well as delivered toys and lived not at the North Pole but in the Laughing Valley of Hohaho.

As stories about Santa grew, it became more common for there to be communication with the merry elf himself. Writing to Santa has been a task eagerly undertaken by many children for years – usually to ask for copious amounts of presents. For more than 20 years, between 1920 and 1943, the children of J.R.R. Tolkien (author of *The Lord of the Rings*) received letters from the North Pole, from Father Christmas himself. Beautifully illustrated and delivered in various ways, they told wonderful stories of mischief and disaster, adventure and battles – how the reindeer got loose and scattered presents all over the place, and how the accident-prone polar bear climbed the North Pole and fell through the roof of Father Christmas's house.

Saturnalia

An ancient Roman festival of Saturn in December. A period of unrestrained merrymaking.

————————————

On 17 December each winter ancient Rome would erupt into a wild party called Saturnalia that lasted seven days. It was in honour of Saturn, the god of agriculture, from whose name we get Saturday. This day in December was the winter solstice and the belief was that this showed spring was drawing near and so the god of agricultural growth needed to be honoured. Saturn was the oldest and most benign deity in ancient Italy and was fabled to have reigned during the Golden Age. This was believed by the Romans to be an era in which plenty abounded and nothing had appeared to corrupt and mar the peace and happiness of humankind. But since that time the world had gone from bad to worse. The desire for gold had brought disastrous evils. As the Saturnalia returned each year it brought with it thoughts of the peaceful reign of Saturn long ago, when all people were happy and good.

During Saturnalia people ate big dinners, and visited their friends with cries of 'Jo Saturnalia!' Their halls were decked with boughs of laurel and green trees, with lighted candles and lamps, and the streets were ablaze with lights and brimming with noisy processions. Bonfires were lit in high places to strengthen the reviving sun in his course. Houses and streets were decorated with flowers and shrubs, and people gave gifts to one another. Life was often turned upside down during this festival. The people governed the rulers, the rich fed the poor and masters wore the garments of slaves. No one could be convicted of a crime over this period.

While there was (and still is) much disagreement about the precise date of Jesus' birth, Pope Julius I (337–52) chose 25 December. It is commonly believed that the church chose this date in an effort to replace the traditions of the pagan Saturnalia festival. By holding Christmas at the same time as traditional winter solstice festivals, church leaders increased the chances that Christmas would be popularly embraced, although they also gave up the ability to dictate how it was celebrated. By the Middle Ages Christianity had, for the most part, replaced pagan religion.

Saviour

*A person who saves someone or something from
danger or harm.*

Origin: from Late Latin salvare, meaning 'to save'.

*The Saviour – yes, the Messiah, the Lord – has been born today in
Bethlehem, the city of David! (Lk. 2.11)*

The word 'saviour' is found in the Bible 39 times and Jesus' actual name means 'God is salvation'. The word 'salvation' is used often in Christianity to explain what God did for humankind by sending his son Christ Jesus.

There is a very personal note in the Christmas message, which is frequently missed by many. The birth of Jesus is not simply an interesting fact of history. Have you ever thought that it was for you the Saviour was born? Jesus was God's Christmas gift to you. As with all gifts, you have a choice whether to accept or reject the gift of salvation.

We cannot understand Jesus if we look just at the baby in the manger. We will also not get a full picture if we just look at the radical life and teachings of this man. Jesus Christ came to earth to die. It looked as if Jesus' life had been a failure, but this was actually part of God's mysterious plan. God the Father allowed Jesus his Son to die for the sins (or wrongdoings) of humans past, present and future; and Jesus was willing to die in our place. He did this so that we could experience forgiveness and enjoy life with God in this life and for eternity. Amazingly, he died so that we don't have to.

Scrooge

A person who is mean with money.

Origin: from the name of Ebenezer Scrooge, a miser in Charles Dickens' A Christmas Carol.

———————

Charles Dickens created a prototype for Scrooge in a tale called *The Story of the Goblins who Stole a Sexton*. Dickens wrote about a grouchy gravedigger called Gabriel Grub who, on his way to dig a grave on Christmas Eve, heard a boy singing a Christmas song. He cheered himself up by striking the child on the head with his lantern a few times and proceeded to the graveyard where he completed his digging. Then a host of goblins appeared and the terrified Grub leapt over tombstones to get away, until a goblin king pulled the gravedigger under the earth. There Grub found himself in an underground cave, the back of which was concealed by a thick cloud. When the cloud rolled away Grub saw scenes of how others spent Christmas. He watched a poor but happy family welcome their father home from work, and other scenes where people courageously persevered through adversity. 'Above all, he saw that men like himself, who snarled at the mirth and cheerfulness of others, were the foulest weeds on the fair surface of the earth.' He awoke a changed man.

In *A Christmas Carol*, published seven years later in 1843, Dickens transformed Grub into Scrooge. Ebenezer Scrooge is a penny-pinching miser of the first degree. He cares nothing for the people around him and others exist only for the money that can be made through exploitation and intimidation. He particularly detests Christmas, which he views as 'a time for finding yourself a year older, and not an hour richer'.

Scrooge is visited on Christmas Eve by the ghost of his former partner Jacob Marley, who died seven Christmas Eves earlier. Marley, a miser from the same mould as Scrooge, is suffering the consequences in the afterlife and hopes to help Scrooge avoid his fate. He tells Scrooge that three spirits will haunt him. These three spirits, the ghosts of Christmas past, present and future, succeed in showing Scrooge the error of his ways. His glorious reformation complete, Christmas morning finds Scrooge sending a Christmas turkey to his long-suffering clerk Bob

Cratchit, and spending Christmas Day in the company of his nephew Fred, whom he had earlier spurned.

Scrooge's newfound benevolence continues as he raises Cratchit's salary and vows to assist his family, which includes Bob's crippled son Tiny Tim. In the end Dickens reports that Scrooge became 'as good a friend, as good a master, and as good a man, as the good old city knew'.

Scrooge is one of the great characters of English literature. A stage villain of Victorian melodrama, he arouses a curious ambiguity in the reader's attitude towards him. How is it that this cruel, selfish old man has such a dynamic appeal to one's sympathy? Is it simply that he is transformed into a generous man at the story's end? Dickens manages the daunting task of presenting his hero in a manner that allows the reader to hiss the villain and relish his presence at the same time.

A Christmas Carol is built on numerous contrasts: rich and poor, warmth and cold, plenty and hunger, family and loneliness, generosity and miserliness, affection and cruelty, dream and reality, freedom and compulsion, past and present, present and future. Most of these opposing forces are recapitulated within the character of Scrooge himself. The cold-hearted, compulsive, lonely, miserly man who eats his meals in the shadows emerges from his dreams, memories and fears into a generous, fun-loving, warm, caring, fatherly man. The texture of the story, rich with contrasting imagery, prepares the reader for Scrooge's conversion well in advance of the concluding chapter.

Shepherd

A person who tends sheep.

At the time of Jesus' birth, communities were very dependent on farming. If too many lambs were lost the community suffered, and with the flocks threatened by wild dogs, wolves and lions it was important for shepherds to be out protecting their flocks.

Sheep were important to the people of Palestine because they provided milk, wool and meat. Shepherds needed to be skilful, resourceful and familiar with the land where the sheep grazed. In the Bible a shepherd was much more than a lowly worker. Shepherds represented leaders of people, someone to guide and ensure their 'flocks' were well and protected. David, later to become the greatest King of Israel, began life as a shepherd on the outskirts of Bethlehem. There was something important about these simple workers that God loved and wanted to use. Indeed, Jesus referred to himself as the 'Good Shepherd'.

The famous hymn 'While Shepherds Watched' talks about the appearance of the angels to the shepherds and their jubilation at the birth of Christ. In 1799 Nahum Tate and Nicholas Brady were associated with creating the new version of the original carol from 1556.

> *While shepherds watched their flocks by night,*
> *All seated on the ground,*
> *The angel of the Lord came down,*
> *And glory shone around.*

While the shepherds are out in the field watching their flocks, the Lord's angel appears to them to bring the exciting news of Jesus' birth. God could just as easily have sent the angel to the political leaders of the day. They could have gathered a great envoy, along with a magnificent military escort, to parade to the location where the mighty Saviour had been born. But they would have been disappointed to see this baby wrapped in blankets in a place where the animals slept, and to discover that the father was only a carpenter and the mother a simple peasant. They might have sneered in mock anger, much like they would years later at an illegal trial and an immoral crucifixion.

If God did not choose the political giants, then why did he not choose the religious leaders? After all, they were trained in the Scriptures, and should have known all about the coming Messiah. But if the religious leaders rejected the messianic claims of the adult Jesus, can you imagine how they would have scoffed at the possibility of a Messiah in a manger?

God often chooses ordinary, down-to-earth people to be his agents, maybe because they are more willing to listen.

Sleigh

A sledge drawn by horses or reindeer.

Origin: from Mid Low German sledde, *related to 'slide'.*

In 1822 Clement Clarke Moore, an Episcopal minister, wrote a long Christmas poem for his three daughters entitled 'An Account of a Visit from St Nicholas'. Moore's poem, which he was hesitant to publish, is largely responsible for our modern image of Santa Claus as a 'right jolly old elf' with a supernatural ability to ascend up a chimney.

Moore's poem helped to popularize the now familiar idea of a Santa Claus who flew from house to house on Christmas Eve in 'a miniature sleigh' led by eight flying reindeer, leaving presents for deserving children.

In 1948 Leroy Anderson wrote the famous carol, 'Sleigh Ride'.

Just hear those sleigh bells jingling,
Ring-ting-tingling too.
Come on, it's lovely weather
For a sleigh ride together with you . . .

Solstice

The two times in the year, respectively at midsummer and midwinter, when the sun reaches its highest or lowest point in the sky at noon, marked by the longest and shortest days.

Origin: from Latin solstitium, *from* sol, *meaning 'sun', and* sistere, *meaning 'stop, be stationary'.*

Religious people worldwide observe many seasonal days of celebration during the month of December. Most are holy days, and are linked in some way to the winter solstice.

The seasons of the year are caused by the 23.5° tilt of the earth's axis. Because the earth is rotating like a spinning top it points in a fixed direction continuously, towards a point in space near the North Star. But the earth is also revolving around the sun. During half the year the southern hemisphere is more exposed to the sun than the northern hemisphere. During the rest of the year the reverse is true. At noon in the northern hemisphere the sun appears high in the sky during summer and low in the sky during winter. The time of the year when the sun reaches its maximum elevation occurs on the day with the greatest number of daylight hours. This is called the summer solstice, and is typically on 21 June, the first day of summer. The lowest elevation occurs around 21 December and is called the winter solstice, when the night-time hours are at their maximum.

In prehistoric times winter was a very difficult time for aboriginal people in the northern latitudes. The growing season had ended and the tribe had to live off stored food and whatever animals they could catch. The people would be troubled as the life-giving sun sank lower in the sky each noon. They feared that it would eventually disappear and leave them in permanent darkness and extreme cold. After the winter solstice they would have reason to celebrate as they saw the sun rising and strengthening once more. Although many months of cold weather remained before spring, they took heart that the return of the warm season was now inevitable. The concept of birth, death and rebirth became associated with the winter solstice. The aboriginal people had no elaborate instruments to detect the solstice, but they were able to notice a slight elevation of the sun's path within a few days after the solstice and celebrations were often on 25 December.

The exact date and time of the solstice varies from year to year and may occur between 20 and 23 December. Below are the predicted dates and times for the coming few years.

Year	Day	Time
2005	21 Dec	18:30
2006	22 Dec	00:20
2007	22 Dec	06:09
2008	21 Dec	11:59
2009	21 Dec	17:49
2010	21 Dec	23:38

Snow

Atmospheric water vapour frozen into ice crystals and falling in light white flakes or lying on the ground as a white layer.

Every year around Christmas, eager yet anxious faces peer out of windows up and down the land, scanning the heavens for a weather change bringing the promise of snow. Yet common sense, and certainly the statistics, would tell us that a true 'Christmas card' scene on the morning of 25 December is most unlikely in most populated areas of the UK.

As far as I'm concerned, if I look out of the window on Christmas Day morning and see a complete covering of snow, then it's a white Christmas. However, the 'official' rules for a white Christmas are very different. If there were three feet of snow on the ground on Christmas morning, but that resulted from a blizzard some six days earlier, and no snow had fallen on Christmas Day itself, then that is not a 'white Christmas' event. But if only a single flake is recorded at a weather centre just five minutes before midnight on Christmas Day, that would be a 'white Christmas' event.

It was Bing Crosby's song that made the phrase 'white Christmas' famous. Crosby was an all-round actor, and in 1942 he starred in the film *Holiday Inn*. In the Christmas holiday section of the film, Irving Berlin composed the song 'White Christmas', which took only 18 minutes to record and at one point was going to be left out altogether. Sales figures of over 100 million for the single version (by all artists) are recorded, and the Crosby version accounts for at least 30 million of these. Until 1997 Crosby's recording of 'White Christmas' was the all-time top-selling single.

Snowmen were probably first made by people to scare away evil winter spirits. Now they are just a good excuse to have lots of fun in the snow. Probably the most famous snowman is Frosty the Snowman, who appears in a Christmas song of the same name, written by Steve Nelson and Jack Rollins in 1950. It was recorded in 1953 by the American singer Perry Como and became very popular. A film called *Frosty the Snowman* was made in 1969 and told the story of a magical snowman who came to life and became best friends with a little girl. In the UK there is a famous animated film called *The Snowman*, about a snowman that comes to life and takes a little boy flying off to see Father Christmas. The film is shown every year on British television and includes a song called 'We're Walking in the Air' sung by choirboy Aled Jones.

The largest snowman in the world was made in Bethel, Maine, USA on 17 February 1999. It was 113ft, 7.5in (35.5m) high and was called 'Angus' after Bethel's town mayor. The thickest bit of ice that scientists have measured by using radio echo soundings was 2.97 miles (4.8km) thick, and was found in Antarctica. The most amount of snow to fall in 12 months was on Mt Baker, Washington State, USA. It fell in the winter of 1998–99 and reached a total of 1,140in – 95ft (29m).

Stamps

A small adhesive piece of paper recording payment of postage.

The first stamp was created in Great Britain in 1840 and was called a 'Penny Black'. This was at the suggestion of a pamphlet entitled *Post Office Reform*, published in 1837 by Rowland Hill. In response to the highly priced and inefficient postage system then in use, he proposed a uniform postage rate of 1d – one penny – across the entire country. He also proposed that by using a specially designed adhesive label to prepay the postage, huge labour costs would be saved. This was known as the Uniform Penny Post scheme, and came into force on 10 January 1840. On the first day of the Penny Post 112,000 letters were posted, more than three times the number posted on that day the previous year. Stamps and printed envelopes and covers became available in May 1840.

The first Christmas stamp was issued in Canada in 1898. On the stamp the words 'XMAS 1898' were inscribed above the background of an ancient map of the world. This was also the year that Canada made the move to adopt the Imperial Penny Postage rate on Christmas Day.

Countries were slow to issue specifically designed Christmas stamps. The next nation with Christmas stamps was Austria in 1937, with two stamps referred to in the Stanley Gibbons catalogue as 'Christmas Greeting Stamps'. Brazil issued four semi-charity stamps in 1939 depicting the three kings and the star, an angel and child, a Southern Cross and child, and mother and child. Hungary was next with a 'Soldier's Christmas' semi-postal depicting a soldier and emblem (1941).

It would be ten years before Cuba issued its two-stamp set of 'Poinsettia' and 'Bells'. Haiti followed in 1954 with two stamps, 'Fort Nativity' and 'Star of Bethlehem'. As the 1950s progressed, Luxembourg and Spain produced Christmas stamps in 1955, while Liechtenstein, Korea and Australia started what has become a fashion with Christmas issues in 1957. The US got on the roll in 1962 with its four-cent 'Wreath and Candles' stamp, a tradition with the US post office that has not been broken since.

Star of Bethlehem

Star: a self-luminous celestial body consisting of gas, viewed from earth as a bright white point in the night sky.

The Star of Bethlehem is recorded in Matthew's Gospel, which states:

> *Jesus was born in Bethlehem in Judea, during the reign of King Herod. About that time some wise men from eastern lands arrived in Jerusalem asking, 'Where is the newborn king of the Jews? We saw his star as it rose, and we have come to worship him.' (Mt. 2.1–2)*

In 1603 Johannes Kepler, imperial mathematician and astronomer to the Holy Roman Empire, observed the 'coming together' of the planets Saturn and Jupiter. Obviously they did not literally come together as they are millions of miles apart, but the light from the planets appeared to merge into a very bright star. Kepler thought that perhaps this is what had happened over 1,600 years earlier at the birth of Christ. His astronomical tables clearly showed that there had been a conjunction of Jupiter and Saturn in 6 BC. To support this theory the translations of the Babylonian School of Astronomy in Sippar, confirmed a conjunction around 7 BC, which was around when Jesus was born.

Modern astronomy can add even more to this theory. Calculations show that the conjunction appeared four times in ten months, first in May in 7 BC, again on 3 October and 4 December of the same year, and at the end of January in 6 BC. Perhaps the Jewish astrologers ('Magi'), who could have been studying at the Sippar school, witnessed the conjunction and saw this to be in line with the ancient tradition that the coming of the Messiah would be heralded by such an event.

Other suggested explanations for the star seen by the wise men are a comet, the birth or death of a star, or even the sighting of the then unknown planet Uranus. Yet others believe it was a new star sent by God, defying the rules of astronomy and science, and once the star had revealed its purpose to the wise men it disappeared and therefore cannot be traced.

Stir-Up Sunday

The Sunday before Advent.

Traditionally Stir-Up Sunday was when Christmas puddings were made, five weeks before Christmas. The collect for that Sunday in the *Book of Common Prayer* of the Church of England, as it was used from the sixteenth to the mid-twentieth centuries, reads:

> *Stir up, we beseech thee, O Lord, the wills of thy faithful people; that they, plenteously bringing forth the fruit of good works, may by thee be plenteously rewarded; through Jesus Christ our Lord. Amen.*

The word 'beseech' means 'arouse, excite, provoke, stimulate, urge'. Church leaders of the past associated the stirring of fruit with the need to ask God to fire into action our wills and desires, to 'stir us up'. The cry to 'stir up' was a reminder to congregations to get their Christmas puddings made in plenty of time to mature before Christmas, but also to get their lives sufficiently 'stirred up' for God.

Every household used to have its own recipe for Christmas pudding, preferably handed down through the generations. It is probable that there were also regional variations. Important additions to the mixture were a coin, a ring and a thimble – the coin to bring good fortune, the ring a marriage and the thimble a life of blessedness.

Apparently, to be made correctly, the pudding should be stirred from east to west in honour of the three wise men. Each family member should give the pudding a stir and make a secret wish or prayer.

Stockings

*A real or ornamental stocking hung up by children on
Christmas Eve for Father Christmas to fill with presents.*

Origin: from 'stock', to supply goods or materials.

It is not certain where the origins of the 'stocking' tradition lie.
According to a variation of the St Nicholas legend, a nobleman grew
despondent over the death of his beloved wife and foolishly squandered
his fortune. This left his three young daughters without dowries and
facing a life of spinsterhood. The generous St Nicholas, hearing of the
girls' plight, set forth to help. Wishing to remain anonymous, he rode his
white horse past the nobleman's house and threw three small pouches of
gold coins down the chimney, where they were fortuitously caught by the
stockings the young women had hung by the fireplace to dry.

Others believe the practice of hanging stockings began during the
sixteenth century in Holland. Children would leave their clogs outside the
front door to be filled with goodies from 'Sintirklass'. Over the years, the
clogs were replaced with Christmas stockings.

The contents of these stockings have also adapted over time. Unlike
today, when parents struggle to get their children to eat fruit, children
used to consider it a rare treat to find an orange in their stocking. Many
continue to receive an orange and a nut as part of the surprise, but on top
of this they have far more high-tech gismos and toys to play with on
Christmas Day.

Henry Livingston set the scene perfectly in his well-known poem:

> 'Twas the night before Christmas, when all through the house
> Not a creature was stirring, not even a mouse;
> The stockings were hung by the chimney with care,
> In hopes that St Nicholas soon would be there.

Whatever the legend, finding a brimming stocking on Christmas morning
is magical.

Television

A system for converting visual images, with sound, into electrical signals, transmitting them by radio or other means, and displaying them electronically on a screen.

One of the reasons why families tend to spend part of Christmas Day watching television is because there is very little publicly arranged entertainment available. Public transport is virtually nonexistent and apart from restaurants and bars there is little to tempt the public outside. Sporting fixtures seldom happen on Christmas Day and so for many home entertainment through television has filled the gap.

In a *Mail on Sunday* survey in which 504 adults were questioned, 76 per cent said they watched television over the Christmas period, whereas only 28 per cent played board games. Eighteen per cent played computer games, but only 7 per cent played charades.

The arrival of digital television has brought abundant choice of programmes to our living rooms in the festive season. Soaps have their most dramatic storyline unravelled on Christmas Day. Movies have also been a central part of the family Christmas since the development of the television in the mid-twentieth century. Some films are repeated every year without fail, for example *The Snowman*, *Scrooge*, *The Sound of Music*, and *It's a Wonderful Life*. Usually these films are watched on their own merit, but it has been known for the television to be switched on as an antidote to annoying relatives during the Christmas season!

Frank Lloyd Wright, the American writer (1867–1959) commented: 'Television is chewing gum for the eyes.' It certainly is.

Tia Maria

*Coffee-flavoured liqueur based on rum,
made originally in the Caribbean.*

Origin: from Spanish Tia Maria, *meaning 'Aunt Mary'.*

The thirteenth-century alchemist Raymond Lully described liqueurs as 'a divinely inspired gift from heaven'. What could be more appropriate to drink during the festive season?

Top-quality liqueurs generally contain around 40 per cent alcohol by volume. Speciality spirits and liqueurs can be served by themselves, before a meal as an aperitif, accompanying the meal, as part of the meal in a dessert or sauce and, of course, with coffee.

The history of liqueurs, also called cordials, is as rich and deep as the flavours that define their character. The alchemists of the late 1200s were the first producers of liqueurs. Believing that these potions had life-giving and healing properties, they appropriately referred to them as *aqua vitae* – 'the water of life'.

Gradually people began to realize that liqueurs were pleasurable to drink and production became more widespread. These days, top-quality speciality spirits and liqueurs are an essential component of drinks cabinets in homes and bars throughout the world. History has it that Frederick the Great, King of Prussia from 1740 to 1786, added champagne to his coffee, but not without first adding a touch of mustard. It sounds pretty awful, but it apparently made him happy.

The process of making many of the classic, popular liqueurs is the same now as it was all those years ago. Although specific recipes remain closely guarded secrets, each method blends a selected spirit with fruit, peels, herbs, spices, nuts, seeds and other exotic flavourings. The ingredients are crushed and then soaked in water or alcohol. Then, the key to the process, the resulting liquid is distilled in alcohol, which condenses the liquid to produce the liqueur.

Tinsel

A form of decoration consisting of thin strips of shiny metal foil attached to a length of thread.

Origin: from Old French estincele, *meaning 'to spark', based on Latin* scintilla, *meaning 'spark'.*

In sixteenth-century France tinsel called *lamé* was placed not on Christmas trees but as decorations on soldiers' uniforms. *Lamé* was made by pulling copper wire through small holes until the wire became as fine as human hair. It was then flattened by heavy rollers. Despite efforts by French *lamé*-makers to preserve the secret of this practice, it soon leaked out into Germany.

In 1610 manufacturers in Germany began to make tinsel out of silver. Machines were invented to stretch out the silver into thin strips. *Lametta*, the German name for tinsel, is a diminutive form of the Italian word *lama*, meaning 'blade'. Silver was durable but tarnished quickly, especially with candlelight, and so inventors tried to create tinsel from a mixture of lead and tin. This was unsuccessful because the mixed tinsel tended to be too heavy and prone to breaking, so people reverted to the use of silver until the mid-twentieth century.

According to legend, tinsel originated from a story about a poor woman. In the seventeenth century a sad widow was left with several children to raise and worked very hard to support them. She diligently created a festive Christmas tree to greet the children on Christmas Day, but during the night spiders spun webs through the limbs of her tree. According to legend, the Christ child witnessed the webbing and, knowing the woman would be devastated to find all her work ruined, he changed the webs into silver.

Trees

A woody perennial plant typically with a single stem or trunk growing to a considerable height and bearing lateral branches.

The custom of having a tree as a focal piece during the winter holiday celebrations can be traced back many centuries. The Druids in France and England were concerned with the autumnal loss of leaves on deciduous trees, as they believed the spirit of the tree had deserted it. To lure the spirits back they dressed the tree as attractively as they could. The ancient Egyptians had a custom of bringing branches from palm trees into their homes on the shortest day of the year each December. The Chinese and Hebrews from ancient history had similar traditions.

The fir tree in particular has a long association with Christianity. It began in Germany in the eighth century when St Boniface, who spread Christianity to the German people, came across a group of pagans worshipping an oak tree. St Boniface is said to have cut down the oak tree in anger, whereupon he discovered a young fir tree at its roots and took this as a sign of the Christian faith.

It was not until the sixteenth century, however, that fir trees were brought indoors at Christmas time. The first decorated tree was at Riga in Latvia, in 1510. Martin Luther is said to have decorated a small Christmas tree with candles, to show his children how the stars twinkled through the dark night. This caught on, and by the end of the century German markets began to sell ornaments to hang on Christmas trees, including 'wafers and golden sugar-twists and paper flowers of all colours'.

The Christmas tree first came to England with the Georgian kings who came from Germany in the eighteenth century. Many German merchants living in England decorated their homes with a Christmas tree, but due to a dislike of the German monarchy the idea did not catch on with the British public.

In 1840, the German Prince Albert married Queen Victoria and brought with him his appreciation of the Christmas tree. As the queen had a much better rapport with the British population, this custom finally became fashionable all around Britain.

As the practice of having a tree grew, people began to realize the potential environmental problems of so many fir trees being cut down during the Christmas season. In response to the damage caused to the forests, the artificial tree was invented in Germany in the 1880s. These trees were initially made of goose feathers, and became increasingly popular in the early twentieth century. In America the Addis Brush Company created the first brush trees, using the same machinery that made their toilet brushes. These had an advantage over the feather tree in that they would take heavier decorations.

In the 1930s there was a revival of Dickensian nostalgia, particularly in Britain. Christmas trees became large, and real again, and were decorated with many bells, balls and tinsels, often with a beautiful golden-haired angel at the top. Although there was a lull during wartime, heavily decorated trees came back straight afterwards.

Further developments of the Christmas tree since then have included the 'silver pine' tree, made of aluminium with a revolving light source underneath for effect. The twentieth century also saw the invention of the fibre-optic Christmas tree where the transmission of light via glass fibres creates a multicoloured, shimmering effect.

Around 60 growers now account for about 6 million Christmas trees that will be bought in the UK every year, with a further 1 million being imported from Denmark and Belgium. Common or Norway spruce (*picea abies*) is the most popular tree in Britain, but the so-called 'designer tree', the Colorado blue spruce (*picea pungens*) with its silvery blue needles, has its own shimmery decorative look and is popular with the style-conscious.

Tree decorations

In the days before electricity, Christmas trees were lit with candles. This practice had obvious dangers. One US newspaper report dated 25 December 1887 described a fire in Matrawan, New Jersey:

> Christmas was a joyous one in the home of Mr Robert Morris . . . until this evening. This evening Mrs Morris decided to light the candles of her Christmas tree, which stood in the front room. Frank, her son, was close behind her as she with matches touched one candle then another. Frank became over anxious and seizing hold of the Christmas tree to see whether one of the candles was alight, he upset the tree. In a moment the whole tree was on fire. The tree in falling, set fire to the house and the house burned down, causing a loss of around $500.

The world's first practical light bulb was invented by Thomas Edison in 1879, and it was to be only three years later that an associate of his, Edward Johnson, lit a Christmas tree electrically for the first time. The tree was in the parlour of his New York home, located in the first section of that city to be wired for electricity. The display created quite a stir and was dutifully recorded in the *Detroit Post and Tribune*:

> Last evening I walked over beyond Fifth Avenue and called at the residence of Edward H. Johnson, vice-president of Edison's electric company. There, at the rear of the beautiful parlour, was a large Christmas tree presenting a most picturesque and uncanny aspect. It was brilliantly lighted with many coloured globes about as large as an English walnut and was turning some six times a minute on a little pine box. There were eighty lights in all encased in these dainty glass eggs, and about equally divided between white, red and blue. As the tree turned, the colours alternated, all the lamps going out and being relit at every revolution. The result was a continuous twinkling of dancing colours, red, white, blue, white, red, blue, all evening. I need not tell you that the scintillating evergreen was a pretty sight, one can hardly imagine anything prettier.

Electric tree lighting was to remain too expensive for the average family for sometime. It only became truly practical when the General Electric Company came to the rescue in 1903. That year the company offered a pre-assembled lighting outfit for the first time at a reasonable price. They were unable to patent their string of lights, and suddenly the market was open for many other companies to manufacture such strings.

Other tree decorations have gone through phases of popularity and sophistication. Initially, in Germany, tree decorations consisted of nuts, fruits, sweets, biscuits and ribbon bows. As things developed, decorations were often homemade. Young ladies spent hours at 'Christmas crafts', quilting snowflakes and stars, sewing little pouches for secret gifts and making paper baskets with sugared almonds in them. Small bead decorations and fine silver tinsel also came from Germany, together with beautiful angels to sit at the top of the tree. By the 1860s the English tree had become more innovative than the delicate trees of earlier decades. Small toys were often hung on the branches, but still most gifts were placed on the table under the tree. By 1900 themed trees were all the rage. During the early twentieth century having as much on the tree as possible was popular, but since then there has been a change of fashion to ensure the tree looks tasteful.

Decorations are often red and green, which are the traditional colours of Christmas. Green represents the continuance of life through the winter months and the Christian belief in eternal life through Jesus Christ, and red symbolizes the blood that Jesus shed at his crucifixion.

Turkey

A large mainly domesticated game bird native to North America, having a bald head and (in the male) red wattles.

The Spanish invaders to South America, known as the 'conquistadors', had discovered turkeys and brought them back to Europe in 1520. It was because these birds were easy to raise and put on weight quickly that they became so popular. Henry VIII was the first English king to enjoy turkey, although it was Edward VII who made eating turkey fashionable at Christmas.

Before turkeys became the popular Christmas choice, peacocks and swans were eaten at celebration meals. To make the roast birds look even richer, medieval cooks added saffron to melted butter and painted the mixture on the meat so it turned golden when cooked. When turkeys were introduced to the Christmas dinner, goose meat was also a very popular alternative. Goose meat is darker than that of the turkey and has a more intense flavour, but today turkey has won the Christmas number one slot.

Before the development of good road and rail links between town and country, turkeys were walked to the market. The turkeys' feet were protected from the frozen mud with 'boots' made from old sacking or leather. The distance from Norfolk, a centre for turkey breeding, to London is 100 miles and the journey would have taken about a week. Whilst turkeys were wild in America, they have to be bred on farms in Europe. It takes about nine months for them to reach a top weight of 36lb (16kg). In the nineteenth century only the white meat from the turkey breast was seen as good enough for guests. The dark meat on the legs would be eaten by the family on the days after Christmas, or given to servants.

Turkey was a luxury right up until the 1950s when refrigerators became commonplace. Today, bred turkeys are either Broad-breasted Bronzes or Beltsville Small Whites. Only male turkeys (toms) gobble. Females (hens) make a clicking noise. The gobble is a seasonal call during the spring and autumn and hens are attracted by the sound for mating.

According to the *Guinness Book of World Records*, the fastest time for plucking a turkey was achieved by Vincent Pilkington of Cootehill, Republic of Ireland, who plucked a turkey in 1 minute 30 seconds on 17 November 1980. Vincent was so enthusiastic about his skills that he even carried out 24 hours of turkey plucking to raise funds for his local school. In this time he plucked 244 turkeys.

On Christmas Day 93 per cent of the population in the UK will eat turkey. This involves the cooking of 11 million turkeys.

Twelfth Night

6 January, the feast of the Epiphany.
Strictly, the evening of 5 January, formerly the twelfth
and last day of Christmas festivities.

Christmas goes out in fine style with Twelfth Night. It is a finish worth of the time. Christmas Day was the morning of the season; New Year's Day the middle of it or noon; Twelfth Night is the night, brilliant with the innumerable plates of Twelfth Cakes. The whole island keeps court; nay all Christendom. The entire world are Kings and Queens. Everybody is somebody else; and learns at once to laugh at, and to tolerate, characters different from his own by enacting them. Cakes, characters, forfeits, lights, theatres, merry rooms, little holiday faces, and, last but not least, the painted sugar on the cakes — all conspires to throw a giddy splendour over the last night of the season.
(Leigh Hunt, Victorian artist)

From the Middle Ages until the nineteenth century, Twelfth Night was actually more popular than Christmas Day. There would be huge parties on Twelfth Night and it was traditional to play practical jokes. These included tricks such as hiding live birds in an empty pie case, so that they flew away when your startled guests cut open the crusts (this is the background to the nursery rhyme 'Sing a Song of Sixpence').

In England the Twelfth Night cake was a rich and dense fruitcake, the ancestor of our modern Christmas cake. This traditionally contained a bean. If you got the bean then you were King or Queen of the Bean and everyone had to do what you told them to do. Sometimes there were also other items in the cake: if you got a clove you were a villain, and if you got a twig you were a fool.

In Scotland until fairly recently a game called Snapdragon was played on Twelfth Night. A large shallow dish would be filled with raisins and a few spoonfuls of brandy poured over them. The lights were then put out and the brandy set alight. People had to snatch the raisins from the flames and make a wish while eating them. Such wishes would then be granted in the next 12 months.

Today in Eastern Orthodox religions, Epiphany (which falls on Twelfth Night) is given more emphasis than Christmas. On this day we remember the visit of the wise men to Jesus. The Twelfth Day also marks the end of the Christian festivals and the traditional time to take down Christmas decorations. In Italy and Spain children still receive gifts on this day in remembrance of the gifts the wise men brought to Jesus. In the Greek Orthodox Church the Blessing of the Waters takes place on 6 January. In this ceremony divers retrieve a cross thrown into the water by a priest.

The 12 days of Christmas

These are the 12 days between Christmas Day and Epiphany, often a national holiday. This would have been a most welcome break for the workers on the land, which in Tudor times would have been the majority of the people. All work, except for looking after the animals, would cease, restarting again on the first Monday after Twelfth Night. This was known as 'Plough Monday' and was the day when ploughmen traditionally blackened their faces and wore white shirts. They would decorate their ploughs and go around collecting money, accompanied by someone acting the Fool. This character would dress in skins and a tail and carried a pig's bladder on the end of a stick.

The famous song 'The 12 Days of Christmas' refers to this holiday period, and was written with a message not always understood today. Catholics in England during the period from 1558 to 1829 were prohibited by a Protestant parliament from any practice of their faith by law, whether in private or public. It was a crime to be a Catholic. 'The 12 Days of Christmas' was written as one of the 'catechism songs' to help young Catholics learn the tenets of their faith. At a time when being caught with anything in writing indicating adherence to the Catholic faith could get you imprisoned or hanged, the song was a memory aid for the principles of the faith.

The gifts in the song have hidden meanings. The 'true love' mentioned in the song refers to God himself. The 'me' who receives the presents refers to every baptized person. The partridge in a pear tree represents Jesus Christ, reigning from the cross (often called a tree in hymns and poems).

These are the rest of the 'hidden' meanings in the song:

2 turtle doves = the Old and New Testaments

3 French hens = faith, hope and charity, the theological virtues

4 calling birds = the four Gospels and the four evangelists, Matthew, Mark, Luke and John

5 gold rings = the first five books of the Old Testament

6 geese a-laying = the six days of Creation

7 swans a-swimming = the seven gifts of the Holy Spirit, the seven sacraments

8 maids a-milking = the eight beatitudes

9 ladies dancing = the nine fruits of the Holy Spirit

10 lords a-leaping = the Ten Commandments

11 pipers piping = the eleven faithful apostles

12 drummers drumming = the twelve points of doctrine in the Apostles' Creed

Umble pie

An animal's entrails, especially those of a deer.

Origin: from 'numbles', from Latin lumbus, *meaning 'loin', as this refers to the back and loins of deer.*

When hunting deer was a popular sport amongst noblemen, in keeping with the spirit of Christmas a decent lord might let the poor have what was left of the deer after the best meat had been removed. These parts were called the 'umbles' and included the heart, liver, tongue, feet, brain and ears. These were mixed with stewing beef, bacon, oysters, rabbit or hare, topped with a layer of dried fruit and baked in a pastry case to form a pie. By the seventeenth century it had become a traditional Christmas dish.

It was always the servants and huntsmen who ate the umble pie, however, not the noblemen. Lord, ladies and guests would have eaten the flesh of the deer, the best part. From this we get the phrase 'to eat humble pie', which means that someone who has come down in life is forced to give way to others in higher positions.

Virgin conception

The doctrine of Christ's birth from a mother,
Mary, who was a virgin.

Origin: from Latin virginem, *meaning 'unwedded maiden'.*

Centuries before the birth, the prophet Isaiah described how God's Son, Jesus Christ, would be born. 'The virgin will conceive a child! She will give birth to a son and will call him Immanuel (which means "God is with us")' (Isa. 7.14).

The New Testament says quite simply that Jesus was conceived in the womb of his mother Mary by a miraculous work of the Holy Spirit and without a human father. Matthew tells us, 'This is how Jesus the Messiah was born. His mother, Mary, was engaged to be married to Joseph. But . . . while she was still a virgin, she became pregnant through the power of the Holy Spirit' (1.18).

Shortly after that an angel of the Lord said to Joseph, 'Joseph, son of David . . . do not be afraid to take Mary as your wife. For the child within her was conceived by the Holy Spirit' (1.20). Then we read that 'when Joseph woke up, he did as the angel of the Lord commanded and took Mary as his wife. But he did not have sexual relations with her until her son was born. And Joseph named him Jesus' (1.24–5).

The same fact is affirmed in Luke's Gospel, where we read about the appearance of the angel Gabriel to Mary. After the angel had told her that she would bear a son, Mary said, 'How can this happen? I am a virgin' (Lk. 1.34). The angel answered, 'The Holy Spirit will come upon you, and the power of the Most High will overshadow you. So the baby to be born will be holy, and he will be called the Son of God' (Lk. 1.35).

The Roman Catholic tradition has it that Mary herself was not of ordinary human nature; that in a similar way to Jesus she was 'immaculate' and absolutely pure. This idea is not documented in the Nativity accounts, but is a belief that developed a few centuries after the birth of Christ. To ignore Mary's humanity entirely, however, would nullify the beautiful arrangement painted through Scripture whereby Jesus is both the son of man and the Son of God.

Wassailing

*Wassail: a toast given to good health at festivities,
especially during Twelfth Night and Christmas Eve.*

Origin: from Middle English waes hail,
meaning 'to your health'.

At gatherings in the Middle Ages, while a bowl of potent brew was handed round, the phrase 'waes hail' – to your health – would be used as a toast, and the recipient would respond with the words 'drinc hail', meaning 'a drink to your health'. Eventually the original phrase evolved into 'wassail' and was used to denote the whole ritual.

As the ritual became more established, households set aside special wassail bowls. The brew was often a mixture of ale, eggs, spices (nutmeg and ginger), honey, cream and roasted apples. Pieces of roasted apple or toast often floated on top of the drink. The first person to have a sip would take out the first piece of toast and wish everyone good health. This is where we get the phrase 'to make a toast' from.

In the late sixteenth or early seventeenth century a new form of wassailing developed. Poor people would go round the households of the wealthy with a filled wassail bowl and after singing carols they would ask for hospitality, a gift, food or money in return for a taste from the wassail bowl.

Wonder

Feeling of surprise and admiration, caused by something
beautiful, unexpected or unfamiliar.

Wonder is key to Christmas. We find it in the eyes of children in shops, as they visit Santa, or when they first see their Christmas stocking overflowing with presents. For adults there is wonder at the atmosphere of a candlelit carol service, at an impressive display of Christmas lights, or at an inspiring story of someone who has helped others at Christmas.

There is also a unique wonder at the beauty of Christ's birth. It is a matter of amazement and awe that God in all his power chose to send his Son Jesus to earth as a humble and helpless baby, in order that he would experience human life fully and would eventually rescue us from darkness.

We have a lot to learn from children. So often as we grow up we lose our sense of wonder. Everything is so new for a child, so exciting, so special, so full of endless possibilities and fun. We can let ourselves become too easily hardened by our pride, by our 'know it all, seen it all before' mentality. In a similar way we can lose our wonder at the idea that God would come from eternity into time, from spirit into flesh. The historian and essayist Thomas Carlyle (1795–1881) wrote, 'Wonder is the basis of worship.'

Wreath

An arrangement of flowers, leaves or stems fastened in a ring and used for decoration or for laying on a grave.

Origin: related to 'writhe', from Old English writhan, meaning 'make into coils, plait'.

There are two types of Christmas wreath, those used during Advent and those used as a decoration in the home. Wreaths were first created in ancient cultures to adorn the bonnets of the rich and royal. In Persia, Partha and Greece the wreath was known as a 'diadem', from the Greek word *diadema*, meaning 'thing bound around'. A diadem worn on the head or bonnet in these cultures was a symbol bearing royal and even spiritual significance.

There is evidence of pre-Christian Germanic peoples using wreaths with lit candles during the cold and dark December days as a sign of hope for the forthcoming warmer and lighter days of spring. In Scandinavia during winter lighted candles were placed around a wheel, and prayers were offered to the god of light to turn 'the wheel of the earth' back toward the sun in order to lengthen the days and restore warmth. A wreath made with holly and mistletoe might also be intended to shelter a home from the spirits of cold and winter.

By the Middle Ages the Christians had adapted this tradition and used wreaths with candles in Advent as part of their preparation for Christmas. After all, Christ is 'the Light that came into the world' to dispel the darkness of sin and to radiate the truth and love of God. Candles are often placed in an Advent wreath and used in church to count down the weeks to Christ's coming.

Wreaths have many other symbolic meanings too. They are made of various evergreens, signifying continuous life. The laurel signifies victory over persecution and suffering; pine, holly and yew represent immortality; cedar means strength and healing. Holly also has a special Christian symbolism as the prickly leaves remind us of Christ's crown of thorns. The circle of the wreath, which has no beginning or end, symbolizes the eternity of God, the immortality of the soul and the everlasting life found in Christ.

Wreaths have been used as a decorative sign of Christmas for hundreds of years. Christmas wreaths can adorn any part of the home, but it is most common to find them on doors, over the mantelpiece or hung in windows.

Xmas

The short form of 'Christmas', the word 'Xmas' began as an abbreviation for church records and charts. The first letter of the word 'Christ' in Greek (*Kristos*) is *chi*, which is identical to our X. Therefore X stands for Christ, as in Xmas. For the early Christians, most of whom spoke and wrote Greek, the word 'Xmas' signified 'Christ's Mass'. The shortening of 'Christmas' to 'Xmas' has been a common practice since the sixteenth century.

Some people condemn the use of the abbreviation as it is believed that the letter X is a secular replacement for 'Christ'. This is incorrect. Originally the X was intended to highlight the cross of Christ, and people using the abbreviation were remembering Christ's death and celebrating the hope he offered humankind by coming to earth. Used in the original context, the X in 'Xmas' cannot be blasphemous.

In recent years, however, due to the growing secularization of Christmas, people have indeed tried to replace and ignore the name of Christ in the word 'Christmas'. It is always good to go back to the question 'Why?' Why do we celebrate Christmas? Why do we commemorate a man who was born over 2,000 years ago? Why have so many seen this man as the centre point of history? If we skim across the surface of Xmas, forgetting what the X stands for, it is possible that we will miss out on someone who could shed light on the whole of reality.

Yule

Archaic term for Christmas.

Origin: originally applied to a heathen festival lasting 12 days.

———————————

Yule is a Scandinavian word for Christmas. *God Jul*, pronounced 'gudt yool', means 'Good Christmas' in Swedish. Yule was a symbol representing the sun, and Yuletide was a festival celebrating the fact that the days would now begin to get longer and warmer again. From the ninth to the eleventh centuries, Danes controlled much of England. They brought with them their own term for Christmas, which in time became an English synonym. 'Yuletide' came to mean 'the Christmas season'.

Yule log

A large log traditionally burnt in the hearth on Christmas Eve;
A log-shaped chocolate cake eaten at Christmas.

The Celts believed that the sun stood still for 12 days during the winter solstice. To mark this, the Druids would bless a 'Yule log' and keep it burning for 12 days. It was not allowed to go out, as they believed this would bring bad luck to the community.

In seventeenth-century Europe there was a tradition that young men would go into a forest at Christmas and find a special Yule log. It was normally huge, so several men had to carry it back, and the trip was an important part of the festivities. Ash was a popular choice because it burns well and is easily found in northern Europe. One end of the log would be placed in the fireplace with the rest sticking out into the room. The log was expected to burn for 12 hours or 12 days, although it would not be totally consumed and a small part would be carefully preserved for the following Christmas, when it would be used to kindle that year's Yule log. Some people believed the ashes from the special log would protect the house from ghosts.

In Yugoslavia the Yule log was cut just before dawn on Christmas Eve and carried into the house at twilight. The wood itself was decorated with flowers, coloured silks and gold, and then doused with wine and an offering of grain. In an area of France known then as Provencal, families would go together to cut the Yule log, singing as they went. These songs asked for blessings to be bestowed upon their homes, crops and flocks. The people of Provencal called their Yule log the *trefoire* and, with great ceremony, carried the log around the house three times and christened it with wine before it was set ablaze.

With the onset of coal, gas and electricity to heat homes, the popularity of the Yule log went into decline. But, as if to save the tradition, French bakeries transformed the log into a chocolate cake called *Buche de Noel* ('Christmas log'). Nowadays these cakes are often elegant and crafted to look like real logs with marzipan tops and detailed decoration.

Zwarte Piet

A character from Dutch Christmas folklore,
where he is St Nicholas's helper.

In Holland Christmas has traditionally been a predominantly religious festival, and children do not get presents from Santa Claus on Christmas Eve. Instead, the day they look forward to is 5 December, the eve of St Nicholas Day. It is said that on this day St Nicholas sails to the city of Amsterdam in a boat from Spain, accompanied by his helper, Zwarte Piet. Church bells ring as they come ashore. Dutch children are told that Zwarte Piet keeps a record of what they do in a big book. Good children will be given presents, which Zwarte Piet brings down the chimney.

Bibliography

Note: the definitions and etymology of words and phrases are based on information from the *Encyclopaedia Britannica*, *Webster's Revised Unabridged Dictionary*, the *Oxford English Dictionary* and www.etymonline.com.

Count, E., Count, A. and Wakefield, D., 4000 *Years of Christmas – A Gift from the Ages* (Ulysses Press 1997).

Deary, Terry, *Horrible Christmas*, (Scholastic Hippo, 2000).

Dickens, Charles, *The Christmas Books* (OUP, 1954).

Golby, J.M. and Purdue, A.W., *The Making of the Modern Christmas* (Batsford, 1986).

Grudem, Wayne, *Bible Doctrine* (Zondervan, 1999).

Matthews, John, *The Winter Solstice – the Sacred Traditions of Christmas* (Quest Books, 1998).

Miles, C., *Christmas Customs and Traditions* (Dover Publications, 1976).

Pearsall, Judy (ed.), *Oxford Concise English Dictionary* (OUP, 2001).

Poston, Elizabeth (ed.), *The Penguin Book of Christmas Carols* (Penguin Books, 1965).

Segall, Barbara, *The Christmas Tree* (Clarkson Potter, 1995).

Stephenson, Michael, *The Christmas Almanac* (OUP, 1992).

Walsh, Joseph J., *Were They Wise Men or Kings?* (Westminster John Knox Press, 2001).

Zevin, J. and Evans, C. (eds), *Kingfisher Illustrated History of the World* (Kingfisher Books, 1992).